D0054120

ALSO BY MARK R. LEVIN

Ameritopia
Liberty and Tyranny
Rescuing Sprite
Men in Black

THE
LIBERTY
AMENDMENTS

RESTORING THE AMERICAN REPUBLIC

Mark R. Levin

THRESHOLD EDITIONS

New York   London   Toronto   Sydney   New Delhi

Threshold Editions
A Division of Simon & Schuster, Inc.
1230 Avenue of the Americas
New York, NY 10020

First Threshold Editions hardcover edition August 2013

THRESHOLD EDITIONS and colophon
are trademarks of Simon & Schuster, Inc.

For information about special discounts for bulk purchases,
please contact Simon & Schuster Special Sales at
1-866-506-1949 or business@simonandschuster.com.

The Simon & Schuster Speakers Bureau can bring authors to your live event.
For more information or to book an event,
contact the Simon & Schuster Speakers Bureau
at 1-866-248-3049 or visit our website at www.simonspeakers.com.

Designed by Joy O'Meara

Manufactured in the United States of America

1   3   5   7   9   10   8   6   4   2

ISBN 978-1-4516-0627-0
ISBN 978-1-4516-0639-3 (ebook)

To My Beloved Family and Fellow Countrymen

CONTENTS

CONTENTS

THE
LIBERTY
AMENDMENTS

CHAPTER ONE

RESTORING THE
AMERICAN REPUBLIC

I UNDERTOOK THIS PROJECT *not* because I believe the Constitution, as originally structured, is outdated and outmoded, thereby requiring modernization through amendments, but because of the *opposite*—that is, the necessity and urgency of *restoring* constitutional republicanism and *preserving* the civil society from the growing authoritarianism of a federal Leviathan. This is not doomsaying or fearmongering but an acknowledgment of fact. The Statists have been successful in their century-long march to disfigure and mangle the constitutional order and undo the social compact. To disclaim the Statists' campaign and aims is to imprudently ignore the inventions and schemes hatched and promoted openly by their philosophers, experts, and academics, and the coercive application of their designs on the citizenry by a delusional governing elite. Their handiwork is omnipresent, for all to see—

a centralized and consolidated government with a ubiquitous network of laws and rules actively suppressing individual initiative, self-interest, and success in the name of the greater good and on behalf of the larger community. Nearly all will be emasculated by it, including the inattentive, ambivalent, and disbelieving.

The nation has entered an age of *post-constitutional soft tyranny*. As French thinker and philosopher Alexis de Tocqueville explained presciently, "It covers the surface of society with a network of small complicated rules, minute and uniform, through which the most original minds and the most energetic characters cannot penetrate, to rise above the crowd. The will of man is not shattered, but softened, bent, and guided; men are seldom forced by it to act, but they are constantly restrained from acting. Such a power does not destroy, but it prevents existence; it does not tyrannize, but it compresses, enervates, extinguishes, and stupefies a people, till each nation is reduced to nothing better than a flock of timid and industrious animals, of which the government is the shepherd."[1]

Social engineering and central planning are imposed without end, since the governing masterminds, drunk with their own conceit and pomposity, have wild imaginations and infinite ideas for reshaping society and molding man's nature in search of the ever-elusive utopian paradise. Their clumsy experiments and infantile pursuits are not measured against any rational standard. Their piousness and sanctimony are justification enough.

Tocqueville observed further, "It would seem as if the rulers of our time sought only to use men in order to make things great; I wish that they would try a little more to make great men; that they would set less value on the work and more upon the workman; that they would never forget that a nation cannot long remain strong when every man belonging to it is individually weak; and that no form or combination of social polity has yet been devised to make an energetic people out of a community of pusillanimous and enfeebled citizens."[2]

Today Congress operates not as the Framers intended, but in the shadows, where it dreams up its most notorious and oppressive laws, coming into the light only to trumpet the genius and earnestness of its goings-on and to enable members to cast their votes. The people are left lamebrained and dumbfounded about their "representatives'" supposed good deeds, which usually take the form of omnibus bills numbering in hundreds if not thousands of pages, and utterly clueless about the effects these laws have on their lives. Of course, that is the point. The public is not to be informed but indoctrinated, manipulated, and misled.

Congress also, and often, delegates unconstitutionally law-making power to a gigantic yet ever-growing administrative state that, in turn, unleashes on society myriad regulations and rules at such a rapid rate the people cannot possibly know of them, either—and if, by chance, they do, they cannot possibly comprehend them. Nonetheless, ignorance, which is widespread and deliberately so, is no excuse for noncompliance, for which the citizen is heavily fined and severely punished.

Not to be outdone, the current occupant of the Oval Office sees his primary duty as "fundamentally transforming the United States of America."[3] By this, of course, President Barack Obama did not mean a fresh allegiance to the nation's founding principles and a new respect for the Constitution's limits on federal authority, but the converse. He is more blatant and aggressive than his twentieth-century predecessors, but faithfully follows the footsteps of the most transgressive among them. The metamorphosis of the executive branch into an immense institution exercising a conglomeration of powers, including lawmaking and decreeing, is clearly without constitutional origin, a quaint notion mostly derided these days.

Having delegated broad lawmaking power to executive branch departments and agencies of its own creation, contravening the separation-of-powers doctrine, Congress now watches as the president inflates the congressional delegations even further and proclaims repeatedly the authority to rule by executive fiat in defiance of, or over the top of, the same Congress that sanctioned a domineering executive branch in the first place. Notwithstanding Congress's delinquency, but because of it, an unquenched President Obama, in a hurry to expedite a societal makeover, has repeatedly admonished Congress that "[i]f [it] won't act soon to protect future generations, I will!"—that is, if Congress will not genuflect to his demands, and pass laws to his liking, he will act on his own.[4]

And the president has made good on his refrain. On a growing list of matters, he has, in fact, displayed an impressive aptitude for imperial rule. With the help of a phalanx of policy "czars," from immigration, the environment, and labor law to health care, welfare, and energy, the president has exercised his executive "discretion" to create new law, abrogate existing law, and generally contrive ways to exploit legal ambiguities as a means to his ends. He has also declared the Senate in recess when it was not, thereby bypassing the Senate's constitutional "advice and consent" role to install several partisans in top federal posts.

Today this is glorified and glamorized as compassionate progressivism. The Framers called it despotism. In *Federalist* 48, James

Madison, considered the father of the Constitution, wrote, "An ELECTIVE DESPOTISM was not the government we fought for; but one which should not only be founded on free principles, but in which the powers of government should be so divided and balanced among several bodies of magistracy, as that no one could transcend their legal limits, without being effectually checked and restrained by the others."[5]

The third branch of the federal triarchy, the judiciary, is no better. Among the biggest myths is that the men and women of the judiciary, operating under monklike conditions, would dutifully and faithfully focus their undivided mental faculties toward preserving the Constitution. They would apply their expertise, experience, and insight free from the political pressures and biases of elections and the legislative and executive branches of government, and within a narrow scope of authority and purpose. Moreover, it was assumed there was little to fear from this part of government. In *Federalist* 78, Alexander Hamilton explained, "Whoever attentively considers the different departments of power must perceive, that, in a government in which they are separated from each other, the judiciary, from the nature of its functions, will always be the least dangerous to the political rights of the Constitution; because it will be least in a capacity to annoy or injure them."[6] Yet, having seized for itself in the early years of the nation the final word on all matters before it, the Supreme Court with just five of its nine members can impose the most far-reaching and breathtaking rulings on the whole of society, for which there is no effective recourse.

It turns out that justices are also God's children; and being of this world, their makeup consists of actual flesh and blood. They are no more noble or virtuous than the rest of us, and in some cases less so, as they suffer from the usual human imperfections and frailties. And the Court's history proves it. In addition to delivering the routine and, in some cases, exceptional rulings, the Court is responsible for several notorious holdings, including *Dred Scott v. Sandford*[7] (endorsing slavery), *Plessy v. Ferguson*[8] (affirming segregation), and *Korematsu v. United States*[9] (upholding the internment of Americans), among others. During the last eighty years or so, the justices have rewritten sections of the Constitution, including the Commerce Clause (redefining noncommerce as commerce) and the tax provisions (redefining penalties as taxes), to accommodate the vast expansion of the federal government's micromanagement over private economic activity. Moreover, the justices have laced the Court's jurisprudence with all manner of personal policy preferences relating to social, cultural, and religious issues, many of which could have been avoided or deferred.

What was to be a relatively innocuous federal government, operating from a defined enumeration of specific grants of power, has become an ever-present and unaccountable force. It is the nation's largest creditor, debtor, lender, employer, consumer, contractor, grantor, property owner, tenant, insurer, health-care provider, and pension guarantor. Moreover, with aggrandized police powers, what it does not control directly it bans or mandates by regulation. For example, the federal government regulates most things in your bathroom, laundry room, and kitchen, as well as the mortgage you hold on your house. It designs your automobile and dictates the kind of fuel it uses. It regulates your baby's toys, crib, and stroller; plans your children's school curriculum and lunch menu; and administers their student loans in college. At your place of employment, the federal government oversees everything from the racial, gender, and age diversity of the workforce to the hours, wages, and benefits paid. Indeed, the question is not what the federal government regulates, but what it does not. And it makes you wonder—how can a people incapable of selecting their own lightbulbs and toilets possess enough competence to vote for their own rulers and fill out complicated tax returns?

The illimitable regulatory activity, with which the federal government torments, harasses, and coerces the individual's private and economic behavior, is the progeny of a colossal federal edifice with inexhaustible energy for societal manipulation and change. In order to satisfy its gluttonous appetite for programmatic schemes, the federal government not only hurriedly digests the Treasury's annual revenue, funded with confiscatory taxes on a diminishing number of productive citizens, but desserts on the wealth not yet created by generations not yet born with unconstrained indebtedness. And what havoc has this wrought.

The federal government consumes nearly 25 percent of all goods and services produced each year by the American people.[10] Yearly deficits routinely exceed $1 trillion.[11] The federal government has incurred a fiscal operating debt of more than $17 trillion, far exceeding the total value of the annual economic wealth created by the American people, which is expected to reach about $26 trillion in a decade.[12] It has accumulated unfunded liabilities for entitlement programs exceeding $90 trillion, which is growing at $4.6–6.9 trillion a year.[13]

There is not enough money on the planet to make good on the federal government's financial obligations. Hence, the Federal Reserve Board has swung into action with multiple versions of "quantitative easing," which is nothing more than the federal government monetizing its own debt—or buying its own debt—

with a combination of borrowing, issuing itself credit, and printing money amounting to trillions of dollars.[14] Of course, this has
the eventual effect of devaluing the currency, fueling significant
inflation or deflation, and destabilizing the economy at some future point.

But like the laws of physics, there is no escaping the laws of
economics. As these fiscal and monetary malpractices escalate, for
there is no end in sight, the federal government will turn increasingly reckless and demanding, taking an even harder line against
the individual's accumulation of wealth and retention of private
property. For example, when the federal income tax was instituted
one hundred years ago, the top individual income tax rate was
7 percent. Today the top rate is about 40 percent, with proposals to push it to nearly 50 percent. There is also serious talk from
the governing elite about instituting a national value-added tax
(VAT) on top of existing federal taxes,[15] which is a form of sales
tax, and divesting citizens of their 401(k) private pension plans.[16]
Even the rapaciousness of these policies will not be enough to fend
off the severe and widespread misery unleashed from years of prof-
ligacy. Smaller nations such as Cyprus, Spain, and Greece provide
a window into the future, as their borrowing has reached its limit.
Moreover, unable to print money, their day of reckoning is either
looming or arrived. Therefore, bank accounts, other investments,
and wealth generally are subject to governmental impoundment,
sequester, and theft. The individual's liberty, inextricably linked
to his private property, is submerged in the quicksand of a government that is aggregating authority and imploding simultaneously.

What, then, is the answer? Again, Tocqueville offers guidance.
Looking back at the Constitutional Convention some fifty years
afterward, he observed that "it is new in history of society to see

a great people turn a calm and scrutinizing eye upon itself when apprised by the legislature that the wheels of its government are stopped, to see it carefully examine the extent of the evil, and patiently wait two whole years until a remedy is discovered, to which it voluntarily submitted without its costing a tear or a drop of blood from mankind."[17]

It is asking too much of today's governing masterminds and their fanatical adherents to reform the product of their own fatuity—that is, the continuing disassembly of the Constitution and society. After all, despite one credible source after another, both within and outside the federal government, ringing alarm bells about the nation's hazardous track—describing it as unsustainable, desperate, and immoral—they are blinded to reason, experience, and knowledge by their political DNA and ideological invincibility and therefore are intransigent to effective ameliorative steps. They long ago renounced by word and action their adherence to the Constitution's confinements since the Statists' utopia and the Framers' Constitution cannot coexist.

However, it is not asking too much of "a great people [to] turn a calm and scrutinizing eye upon itself" and rally to their own salvation. It is time to return to self-government, where the people are sovereign and not subjects and can reclaim some control over their future rather than accept as inevitable a dismal fate. Unlike the radicalism of the governing masterminds, who self-servingly oversee a century-old, perpetual counterrevolution against the American dawn, the people must have as their goal the reestablishment of the founding principles and the restoration of constitutional republicanism, thereby nurturing the individual and preserving the civil society. This requires, first, an acknowledgment of the federal government's unmooring from its constitutional foundation; second, an acceptance that the condition is urgent and, if untreated, will ultimately be the death knell of the American Republic; third, the wisdom to rebalance the government in a way that is without novelty and true to the Framers' original purpose; and, fourth, the courage to confront— intellectually and politically—the Statists' stubborn grip on power.

There is a path forward but it requires an enlightened look back at our founding. And what we find is that the Framers rightly insisted on preserving the prominent governing role of the state legislatures as a crucial mechanism to containing the power of the proposed new federal government. In fact, other than the limited, specified powers granted to the federal government, the states retained for themselves plenary governing authority. The debates during the Constitutional Convention and the state ratification conventions are unequivocal in this regard. During the ratification period, the Federalists repeatedly assured the Anti-Federalists and other skeptics of the proposed federal government's limits. For example, Madison argued in *Federalist* 14, "In the first place, it is to be remembered, that the general government is not to be charged with the whole power of making and administering laws: its jurisdiction is limited to certain enumerated objects, which concern all the members of the republic, but which are not to be attained by the *separate* provisions of any."[18] In *Federalist* 45 he insisted, "The powers delegated by the proposed Constitution to the federal government are few and defined. Those which are to remain in the State governments are numerous and indefinite."[19] In *Federalist* 46, Madison asserted that "the powers proposed to be lodged in the federal government are as little formidable to those reserved to the individual States, as they are indispensably necessary to accomplish the purposes of the Union; and that all those alarms which have been sounded, of a meditated and consequential annihilation of the State governments, must, on the most favorable interpretation, be ascribed to the chimerical fears of the authors of them."[20]

Madison's declarations were not unique among the Constitution's proponents but rather were commonplace. And without these assurances—and the additional pledge that the First Congress would offer amendments to the Constitution further ensuring that individual and state sovereignty would be safeguarded against the new federal government (what became the Bill of Rights, including the Ninth and Tenth Amendments)—the Constitution would not have been ratified. Thus, the Constitution, drafted by delegates who were sent by the states to Philadelphia in 1787 and ratified subsequently by delegates in the state conventions, preserved the decisive role of the states in the American Republic.

It requires emphasis that *the states* established the American Republic and, through the Constitution, retained for themselves significant authority to ensure the republic's durability. This is not to say that the states are perfect governing institutions. Many are no more respectful of unalienable rights than is the federal government. But the issue is how best to preserve the civil society in a world of imperfect people and institutions. The answer, the Framers concluded, is to diversify authority with a combination of governing checks, balances, and divisions, intended to prevent the concentration of unbridled power in the hands of a relative few imperfect people.

Unlike the modern Statist, who defies, ignores, or rewrites the Constitution for the purpose of evasion, I propose that we, the

people, take a closer look at the Constitution for our preservation. The Constitution itself provides the means for restoring self-
government and averting societal catastrophe (or, in the case of
societal collapse, resurrecting the civil society) in Article V.

Article V sets forth the two processes for amending the Constitution, the second of which I have emphasized in italics:

> The Congress, whenever two thirds of both Houses shall
> deem it necessary, shall propose Amendments to this Con-
> stitution, or, *on the Application of the Legislatures of two
> thirds of the several States, shall call a Convention for proposing
> Amendments*, which, in either Case, *shall be valid to all Intents
> and Purposes, as Part of this Constitution, when ratified by the
> Legislatures of three fourths of the several States or by Conven-
> tions in three fourths thereof*, as the one or the other Mode of
> Ratification may be proposed by the Congress . . .[21]

Importantly, in neither case does the Article V amendment
process provide for a constitutional convention. It provides for
two methods of amending the Constitution. The first method,
where two-thirds of Congress passes a proposed amendment and
then forwards it to the state legislatures for possible ratification
by three-fourths of the states, has occurred on twenty-seven occasions. The second method, involving the direct application of
two-thirds of the state legislatures for *a Convention for proposing
Amendments*, which would thereafter also require a three-fourths
ratification vote by the states, has been tried in the past but without success. Today it sits dormant.

The fact is that Article V expressly grants state legislatures significant authority to rebalance the constitutional structure for the purpose of restoring our founding principles should the federal government shed its limitations, abandon its original purpose, and grow too powerful, as many delegates in Philadelphia and the state conventions had worried it might. The idea was first presented at the Constitutional Convention on May 29, 1787, by Edmund Randolph, governor of Virginia, as a proposal in the so-called Virginia Plan drafted by Madison.

> Resd. that provision ought to be made for the amendment of the Articles of Union whensoever it shall seem necessary, and that the assent of the National Legislature ought not be required thereto.[22]

On June 11, George Mason of Virginia—who had earlier drafted Virginia's Declaration of Rights, the precursor to the Declaration of Independence—responded to some of the delegates who did not see the necessity of the proposal, by strongly advocating for it.

> Col: Mason urged the necessity of such a provision. The plan now to be formed will certainly be defective, as the Confederation has been found on trial to be. Amendments therefore will be necessary, and it will be better to provide for them, in any easy, regular and Constitutional way than to trust to chance and violence. It would be improper to require the consent of the Natl Legislature, because they may abuse their power, and refuse their consent on that very account. . . .[23]

Later, when the delegates returned to the issue, Roger Sherman of Connecticut—who had been a member of the Committee of Five, which helped draft the Declaration of Independence, and who coauthored the so-called Connecticut Plan, which served as the basis for our bicameral Congress—offered an alternative in which Congress would propose amendments and the states would ratify them. Madison suggested dropping the state convention altogether.

On September 15, Mason, alarmed that Congress would have the sole power to propose amendments, continued to insist on state authority to call for conventions. Mason explained that an oppressive Congress would never agree to propose amendments curtailing its own tyranny:

> Col: Mason thought the plan of amending the Constitution exceptionable & dangerous. As the proposing of amendments is in both the modes to depend, in the first immediately, and in the second, ultimately, on Congress, no amendments of the proper kind would ever be obtained by the people, if the Government should become oppressive, as he verily believed would be the case.[24]
>
> Mr. [Gouverneur] Morris [of Pennsylvania] & Mr. [Elbridge] Gerry [of Massachusetts] moved to amend the article so as to require a Convention on application of 2/3 of the Sts [states].[25]

Earlier, Pennsylvania's James Wilson, among the most active participants at the Constitutional Convention, had "moved to insert 'three fourths of' before the words 'several States,' " which was adopted and then ultimately added as a requirement for both amendment processes under Article V.[26] Consequently, under both amendment procedures, the Constitution requires that three-fourths of the states ratify amendments, either by their state legislatures or state conventions.

I was originally skeptical of amending the Constitution by the state convention process. I fretted it could turn into a runaway caucus. As an ardent defender of the Constitution who reveres the brilliance of the Framers, I assumed this would play disastrously into the hands of the Statists. However, today I am a confident and enthusiastic advocate for the process. The text of Article V makes clear that there is a serious check in place. Whether the product of Congress or a convention, a proposed amendment has no effect at all unless "ratified by the Legislatures of three fourths of the several States or by Conventions in three fourths thereof. . . ." This should extinguish anxiety that the state convention process could hijack the Constitution.

After more research and reflection, the issue crystallized further. If the Framers were alarmed that states calling for *a Convention for proposing Amendments* could undo the entire undertaking of the Constitutional Convention, then why did they craft, adopt, and endorse the language? In *Federalist* 43, Madison considered both Article V amendment processes equally prudent and judicious. He wrote, in part, "That useful alterations will be suggested by experience, could not but be foreseen. It was requisite, therefore, that a mode for introducing them should be provided. The mode preferred by the convention seems to be stamped with every mark of propriety. It guards equally against that extreme facility, which would render the Constitution too mutable; and that extreme difficulty, which might perpetuate its discovered faults. It, moreover, equally enables the general and the State governments to originate the amendment of errors, as they may be pointed out by the experience on one side, or on the other. . . ."[27]

There are other reasons for assuaging concerns. Robert G. Natelson, a former professor of law at the University of Montana and an expert on the state convention process, explains that "a convention for proposing amendments is a *federal convention*; it is a creature of the states or, more specifically, of the state legislatures. And it is a *limited-purpose convention*. It is not designed to set up an entirely new constitution or a new form of government. How do we know that it's a federal convention? [It] was the only kind of interstate convention the Founders ever knew, or likely ever considered. Indeed, when they talked during the ratification process about conventions for proposing amendments, they always talked about them as representing the states."[28] Moreover, the state legislatures determine if they want to make application for a convention; the method for selecting their delegates; and the subject matter of the convention.[29]

In addition, Congress's role in the state application process is minimal and ministerial. It could not be otherwise, as the Framers and ratifiers adopted the state convention process for the purpose of establishing an alternative to the congressionally initiated amendment process. It provided a constitutional solution should "the [federal] Government . . . become oppressive."[30] The text and plain meaning of Article V are inarguable. In *Federalist* 85, Alexander Hamilton—a leading advocate of a robust federal government—explained that "the national rulers, whenever nine [two-thirds] States concur, will have no option upon the subject. By the fifth article of the plan, the Congress will be *obliged* 'on the application of the legislatures of two thirds of the States [which at present amount to nine], to call a convention for proposing amendments, which *shall be valid*, to all intents and purposes, as part of the Constitution, when ratified by the legislatures of three fourths of the States, or by conventions in three fourths thereof.' The words of this article are peremptory. The Congress '*shall* call a convention.' Nothing in this particular is left to the discretion of that body. And of consequence, all the declamation about the disinclination to a change vanishes in air."[31]

I have no illusions about the political difficulty in rallying support for amending the Constitution by this process. After all, all past efforts have fallen short. And the governing masterminds and their disciples are more powerful and strident than ever. There is no doubt that their resistance will be stubborn and their tactics desperate as they unleash the instrumentalities of the federal government and the outlets of a corroboratory media to vanquish such a movement and subdue the public. Having rejected the Constitution's limits, they will not be persuaded by references to its text and history. Their evasion has been their design. Others who self-identify as originalists, constitutionalists, and conservatives in asserting allegiance to the Constitution, as I do, might nonetheless be wary of or opposed reflexively to the state convention process for several reasons, including their unfamiliarity with its history and workings. Perhaps, in time, their high regard for the Constitution will persuade them of the judiciousness in resorting to it before there is little left of it. Still more may be resigned to a grim future, preferring lamentation to the hard work of purposeful action. And, of course, there are always the unmindful and content.

Whatever the reasons, there are also untold numbers of citizens who comprehend the perilousness of the times and circumstances, and the urgency of drawing the nation's attention to the restoration of constitutional republicanism. This book is an appeal to them. The Framers anticipated this day might arrive, for they knew that republics deteriorate at first from within. They provided a lawful and civil way to repair what has transpired. We, the people, through our state legislatures—and the state legislatures, acting collectively—have enormous power to constrain the federal government, reestablish self-government, and secure individual sovereignty.

What follows are proposed amendments to the Constitution—*The Liberty Amendments*. It is my hope and aspiration for our country that these amendments can spur interest in and, ultimately, support for the state convention process. In any event, should there come a time, sooner or later, when the states convene a convention, these amendments or amendments of the same nature—as I make no claim of unassailable knowledge—may prove useful and find their way into the debate. But a plan is what is needed, as is a first step. This is mine.

CHAPTER TWO

AN AMENDMENT TO ESTABLISH TERM LIMITS FOR MEMBERS OF CONGRESS

SECTION 1: No person may serve more than twelve years as a member of Congress, whether such service is exclusively in the House or the Senate or combined in both Houses.

SECTION 2: Upon ratification of this Article, any incumbent member of Congress whose term exceeds the twelve-year limit shall complete the current term, but thereafter shall be ineligible for further service as a member of Congress.

IN 2010, THE YEAR of a Republican tidal wave, 85 percent of incumbents from both parties were reelected. Three hundred ninety-seven members of the House of Representatives in the 111th Congress ran for reelection and 339 won. The story in the Senate was almost a mirror image of the House. A third

of the seats in the Senate were up for election. Twenty-five incumbents stood for reelection and twenty-one won. The Senate's
incumbent reelection rate was 84 percent.[1]

In 2008, the year Barack Obama was first elected president,
the reelection percentage for House members was 94 percent. The
Senate's was down a hair to 83 percent. In fact, you can look at
almost any congressional election cycle in the last two decades
and find similar results.[2]

Ronald Rotunda, Chapman University law professor and constitutional expert, made the point a few years ago that "turnover in
the House of Lords has been greater than the turnover in the House
of Representatives. There was even more turnover in the membership of the Soviet Politburo."[3] And little has changed since.

In theory, there is nothing wrong with keeping a good public
servant in office for as long as the official and we, the voters, want
him there. New does not necessarily mean better, and often it can
mean worse. And in our country, where the people regularly get
to vote for members of the House and Senate—within very basic
qualifications like age, citizenship, and residency—whomever
voters choose to represent them should be up to them, right?

The problem is that theory can be a cruel mistress when it
comes to reality, in which unexpected consequences often prevail.
America has never been a pure democracy and majoritarianism
has always been as much feared as monarchism. Moreover, our
supposedly broad parameters of "choice" at the ballot box have
actually caused a dramatic narrowing of electoral options for
voters. Putting aside the media histrionics over "divided" government and the "dysfunctional" relationships between the two
houses of Congress, these institutions are populated by a class of
elected officials who jealously covet the power of public office.

Through gerrymandering of House districts, patronage, a barrage of self-serving free and paid media, and fund-raising advantages, incumbents are able to extend their hold on federal office. Furthermore, incumbents often use their positions as lawmakers to promote federal spending and legal initiatives that benefit their personal longevity in office, making it increasingly difficult for successful electoral challenges. For example, part of the unsustainable growth of the federal government can be attributed to members of Congress treating federal spending, borrowing, and taxing as a personal prerogative used to award funds and assign legal rights to various political and electoral constituencies and would-be constituencies. There are undoubtedly other reasons for their behavior, including and most certainly ideology, but there is no denying that the instrumentalities of the federal government are used to build political constituencies and supporters—that is, to reshape the nature and mind-set of the electorate. Therefore, Congress has become less of a representative body as its members are more insulated.

The consequences of these and other practices addressed by *The Liberty Amendments* have been extremely detrimental to our society, as measured by, among other things, the ever-more-centralized and coercive power of the federal government, unsustainable fiscal and monetary policies, and myriad statutes and regulations issued by a maze of federal departments and agencies. The ultimate costs are borne by the individual in lost liberties and property. Thus, while there are a host of complex circumstances that brought us to our current state, much of it would not be possible but for an increasingly insulated class of governing masterminds who use lawmaking and the public purse to empower themselves. It is apparent that in Washington and most political capitals *TIME* in office = *POWER*.

An important antidote is congressional term limits, which slowly displaces a self-perpetuating ruling class populated by professional politicians—which is increasingly authoritarian in its approach to governance—with a legislative body whose members are, in fact, more representative of the people, for they are rotated in and out of Congress over a generally shorter and defined period of time. University of California, Irvine, professor Mark P. Petracca explains that this rotation of citizen-representatives is central to a republic. "The oft-touted expertise of professional politicians as representatives stands in stark contradiction to the essential function of political representation in a democratic republic, namely, to connect the people to the government through representatives who share their values and stay in touch with the reality of their day-to-day lives."[4] Congressional terms limits alone are not enough to rebalance our governing system, but they are a necessary and critical building block.

Term limits were not included in the Constitution as originally adopted and ratified, but they were recognized commonly as curbing the use and abuse of governmental power at the time of the Constitutional Convention. Benjamin Franklin, the primary author of the Pennsylvania Constitution, included an article preventing anyone from serving in the Pennsylvania General Assembly more than four years out of any seven.[5] The twelve-member executive council for the commonwealth also required that members serve no more than one three-year term, and then be off the council for an additional four years.[6]

In addition, the Articles of Confederation, the first governing document the nascent republic adopted shortly after declaring its independence, also included a restriction on service in the Congress, the unicameral governing body made up of delegates from the thirteen states. Article V of the Articles stated that "no per-son shall be capable of being a delegate for more than three years in any term of six years. . . ."[7]

The prevailing concern at the outset of the Constitutional Convention was that the new central government possess suf-ficient authority to overcome the weaknesses of the Articles of Confederation, but not denude the states of their independent and exclusive authority to administer a broad array of governmen-tal functions. Hence, more attention was focused on devising the "checks and balances" within the federal government and secur-ing state sovereignty through federalism to prevent abuse.

In the Constitutional Convention, on June 2, only days after it convened, Franklin offered his opinion about the question of paying legislators and executive officers of the federal govern-ment. He opposed the idea. But his speech is relevant respecting the effect of power on public officials, which can be read today as a prescient and compelling warning about human behavior.

> Sir, there are two passions which have a powerful influence on the affairs of men. These are ambition and avarice; the love of power and the love of money. Separately each of these has great force in prompting men to action; but when united in view of the same object, they have in many minds the most violent effects. Place before the eyes of such men, a post of honour that shall be at the same time a place of *profit*, and they will move heaven and earth to obtain it. The vast number of such places it is that renders the British Gov-ernment so tempestuous. The struggles for them are the true sources of all of those factions which are perpetually divid-ing the Nation, distracting its Councils, hurrying sometimes

into fruitless & mischievous wars, and often compelling a submission to dishonorable terms of peace.

And of what kind are the men that will strive for this profitable pre-eminence, through all the bustle of cabal, the heat of contention, the infinite mutual abuse of parties, tearing to pieces the best of characters? It will not be the wise and moderate; the lovers of peace and good order, the men fittest for the trust. It will be the bold and the violent, the men of strong passions and indefatigable activity in their selfish pursuits. These will thrust themselves into your Government and be your rulers—And these too will be mistaken in the expected happiness of their situation: For their vanquished competitors of the same spirit, and from the same motives will perpetually be endeavouring to distress their administration, thwart their measures, and render them odious to the people.

Franklin continued:

Besides these evils, Sir, tho' we may set out in the beginning with moderate salaries, we shall find that such will not be of long continuance. Reasons will never be wanting for proposed augmentations. And there will all always be a party for giving more to the rulers, that the rulers may be able in return to give more to them.—Hence as all history informs us, there has been in every State & Kingdom a constant warfare between the governing and the governed: the one striving to obtain more for its support, and the other to pay less. And this has alone occasioned great convulsions, actual civil wars, ending either in dethroning of the Princes, or en-

slaving the people. Generally indeed the ruling power car-
ries its point, the revenues of princes constantly increasing,
and we see that they are never satisfied, but always in want
of more. The more the people are discontented with the
oppression of taxes; the greater the need the prince has of
money to distribute among his partisans and pay the troops
that are to suppress all resistance, and enable him to plun-
der at pleasure. There is scarce a king in a hundred who
would not, if he could, follow the example of the Pharaoh,
get first all the people's money, then all their lands, and then
make them and their children servants for ever. It will be
said, that we don't propose to establish Kings. I know it. But
there is a natural inclination in mankind to Kingly Government. It sometimes relieves them from Aristocratic domination. They had rather have one tyrant than five hundred. It
gives more of the appearance of equality among Citizens,
and that they like. I am apprehensive therefore, perhaps too
apprehensive, that the Government of these States, may
in future times, end in a Monarchy. But this Catastrophe
I think may be long delayed, if in our proposed System we
do not sow the seeds of contention, faction & tumult, by
making our posts of honor, places of profit. . . .[8]

What Franklin was trying to do was use two of the forces that
animate individuals to action, ambition and avarice, to make
federal office unattractive to people who are motivated solely or
primarily by those character traits. In essence, he was arguing for
a de facto term limit on government service by making the act of
service a genuine sacrifice for an incumbent. And that was, and is
more so today, a valid objective.

In fact, as Professor Petracca recounts, there was a tradition of rotation that grew during the American Revolutionary period. "[T]he expectation or requirement that elected officials would soon 'return' to 'private life' or 'private station' was contained in the bills of rights accompanying six of the new state constitutions adopted from 1776 to 1780. The Virginia Bill of Rights . . . provided that members of the legislature and executive 'may be restrained from oppression, by feeling and participating the burdens of the people, they should, at fixed periods, be reduced to private station' (1776, section 5). Similar provisions appeared in the bills of rights accompanying the constitutions of Pennsylvania (1776, articles 19 and 11); Delaware (1776, article 4); New York (1777, article 11); South Carolina (1778, article 9); and Massachusetts (1780, article 8)."[9]

Thomas Jefferson was a longtime proponent of rotation. In a reply letter to James Madison, commenting on the proposed Constitution, he wrote in December 1787, in part, that "I dislike, and strongly dislike . . . the abandonment, in every instance, of the principle of rotation in office, and most particularly in the case of the President. . . ."[10] In February 1800, Jefferson explained to Samuel Adams that "[a] government by representees, elected by the people at short periods, was our object, and our maxim at that day was, 'Where annual election ends, tyranny begins'; nor have our departures from it been sanctioned by the happiness of their effects. . . ."[11]

Numerous delegates to the Constitutional Convention supported rotation in office. And they debated terms of office for each of the newly created public offices. But, as Jefferson pointed out in his letter to Madison, he was concerned that there was no provision in the draft Constitution for mandatory rotation or term limits. However, it would be erroneous to conclude from its absence that the matter of term limits was considered and rejected. The concept of representation at the time was not one of "professional" or lifetime "public service" but citizen participation and part-time service. Moreover, the relatively short terms established for members of the House and the president, and even the six-year term for senators elected by the state legislatures, was thought to ensure a regular and steady turnover of officeholders. And life expectancy was much shorter than today.

As Petracca explains, "throughout most of the nineteenth century, not very many members of Congress sought reelection. Not until 1901 . . . did the average number of terms served by House members prior to the present session rise above two terms. There were few occasions in which the average length of service approached two terms, but no more than a handful out of some 56 sessions. . . . During the 25 elections between 1850 and 1898 . . . turnover averaged 50.2 percent. On average, more than half the House during any given session in the second half of the nineteenth century was made up of first term members."[12]

George Washington's approach to the presidency reflected the mind-set of the period. While there was no constitutional stricture at the time on how many terms a president may serve, Washington set the precedent that reflected both the public's general perception of how long a president should serve—two four-year terms—and how long the body politic would consider someone electable.

This perspective, respecting presidential power in particular, operated for almost a century and a half, until Franklin Roosevelt ran for and won a third term in 1940. He went on to win a fourth term in 1944, but served only a few months of that term before he died in office on April 12, 1945.

Shortly after World War II, when the Republican Party captured control of both houses of Congress, there was strong sentiment that President Washington's precedent of serving only two terms should be codified in order to prevent future presidents from holding power too long. This led to the Twenty-Second Amendment to the Constitution, which was ratified on February 27, 1951.[13] It limits a president to two terms or, in the case of a vice president who has assumed the office because of the death, resignation, impeachment conviction, or disability of a predecessor, two terms and the predecessor's term, if the term is more than half over.[14] A vice president may serve only one term and the remainder of the previous incumbent's term, if that term is less than half completed.[15] Although limiting a president's term of service, Congress did not address the longevity of its own members.

There are really only two ways to curb prolonged incumbency: 1) limit who is eligible to seek and hold a position of power; and/or 2) establish explicit, definitive mechanisms in the operation of government that constrain the power of the officeholder. The Framers attempted to control the purview of the federal government through a carefully balanced retinue of checks on each branch of the federal government's power. These divisions of enumerated authority between the branches meant that no one part of government could dominate the others or subsume the states' power. In this way, the civil society and individual sovereignty could be preserved. The blueprint for this system, the Constitution, was the greatest mechanism for human governance ever created.

The problem today, however, is that we have had a century or more of elected officials who have incrementally dismantled the Constitution's structure, leaving us—as I wrote in *Ameritopia*—in a post-constitutional period. The evidence abounds, and is described at length throughout this book. The nation's Founders believed in the concept of a "citizen/servant"—someone who had a life and a career in the private sector, but who offered his experience and talents to public service for a limited time, and then returned to private life. In many cases, government officials, even representatives and senators, actually kept active in their private sector vocation during their tenure in public office, dividing time between the two areas of life. The size of the national government, as well as its reach, was kept small and intentionally curtailed. Moreover, the notion of a career in elective office, in the context of a constitutional republic, was both foreign and incongruous.

An excellent example of the mind-set of the Founders toward government service was the manner of compensation established for our national elected officials. President Washington's salary was $25,000 per year, plus expenses—a generous but not lavish sum in 1789.[16] There was, however, some debate about a fair wage for his vice president, John Adams. Some in Congress wanted to pay him on a per diem basis, for each day he actually worked at being a heartbeat away from the presidency. After some debate, Congress provided Adams with an annual salary of $5,000.[17]

The First Congress was a bit more penurious with its own compensation. Senators and representatives were given six dollars for each day Congress was actually in session. And up until the beginning of the twentieth century, Congress was seldom in session more than an average of about four months per year. In fact, between the beginning of the First Congress in 1789 and 1855, members of Congress were paid the same six-dollars-per-diem salary—except for 1815–17, when Congress voted itself a $1,500 annual paycheck. After 1855, members were paid $3,000 per year.[18]

The citizenry's basic antipathy against marshaling power in a single individual's hands was also reflected in their choices for president. From 1836 to 1868, only one candidate was elected to the presidency more than once—Abraham Lincoln.

Not surprisingly, the timeline for congressional tenure burgeoned concurrently with the rise of the Progressive movement in the United States. As the Progressives grew in influence in state and federal governments, the federal government—by necessity, from the Progressives' perspective—grew more dominant and intrusive. A top-down centralized government was required to pursue utopian objectives of economic, social, and cultural egalitarianism and reformation. Thus, the adoption of the Sixteenth Amendment and the federal income tax and the repeal of the Seventeenth Amendment and state representation in the Senate, among other things, contributed to the unleashing of infinite and unfinished acts of centralized government. The very nature of representative government under the Constitution, with its structural limits on federal governmental action and respect for individual sovereignty and local community interests denoted in the Ninth and Tenth Amendments, was altered fundamentally. Today it reveals itself in relentless social engineering and lifestyle calibrations.

Consequently, citizen legislators, rotating back to their communities after a short period of public service—considered an indispensable and routine characteristic and design of representative government at the time of the founding, and for a century thereafter—have been replaced with a professional ruling class led by governing masterminds. For the most part, they are isolated from the communities from which they hail and are consumed with the daily jockeying for position and power within their ranks. Moreover, they both pander to and lord over their constituents.

This proposed amendment limits the length of time an individual can serve in Congress to up to a total of twelve years, whether such service is exclusively in one House or combined in both Houses. Beyond that, an incumbent is ineligible to run again. Although imperative to reestablishing the American Republic, this amendment is not extraordinary. Voters are used to the impact of the Twenty-Second Amendment on presidential elections, and thirty-six of the fifty states have some form of term limits for their governors.[19] Some states have limits on the number of terms a governor may serve throughout his life, while others have limits on serving consecutive terms. For example, Virginia prohibits reelection after a single gubernatorial term.[20] Only one state, Utah, has no term limits since the legislature repealed the state's term limits statutes.[21] In addition, fifteen states have term limits for state legislators.[22] There are also term limits on members of several municipal, county, and town governing bodies.

Benjamin Franklin put term limits in the proper context. On July 26, 1787, at the Constitutional Convention, he said: "It seems to have been imagined by some that the returning to the mass of the people was degrading the magistrate. This he thought was contrary to republican principles. In free Governments the rulers are the servants and the people their superiors & sovereigns. For the former therefore to return among the latter was not to *degrade* but to *promote* them. And it would be imposing an unreasonable burden on them, to keep them always in a State of servitude, and not allow them to become again one of the Masters."[23]

The consent of the governed is the hallmark of a constitutional republic. Yet it seems the American people have lost faith in Congress as an institution. Congress, which is supposed to reflect the will of the people better than the other branches of the federal government, is consistently rated very poorly by the citizenry. The level of public disenchantment is significant. Congress's approval averaged 14 percent for the first part of 2013, 15 percent in 2012, 17 percent in 2011, and 19 percent in 2010.[24] The longevity of incumbency has created a class of professional politicians who operate at an increasing distance from their constituents. Term limits, and the more frequent rotation of individuals in and out of Congress, provide a remedy consistent with the Framers' intent and approach to representative government.

CHAPTER THREE

An Amendment to Restore the Senate

SECTION 1: The Seventeenth Amendment is hereby repealed. All Senators shall be chosen by their state legislatures as prescribed by Article I.

SECTION 2: This amendment shall not be so construed as to affect the term of any Senator chosen before it becomes valid as part of the Constitution.

SECTION 3: When vacancies occur in the representation of any State in the Senate for more than ninety days the governor of the State shall appoint an individual to fill the vacancy for the remainder of the term.

SECTION 4: A Senator may be removed from office by a two-thirds vote of the state legislature.

An amendment to the U.S. Constitution that was sold as a cleansing and transformative expansion of popular democracy is actually an object lesson in the malignancy of the Progressive mind-set and its destructive impact on the way we practice self-government in a twenty-first-century, post-constitutional nation.

The amendment in question is the Seventeenth, ratified April 8, 1913. Its language is deceptively uncomplicated:

> The Senate of the United States shall be composed of two Senators from each State, elected by the people thereof, for six years; and each Senator shall have one vote. The electors in each State shall have the qualifications requisite for electors of the most numerous branch of the State legislature.
>
> When vacancies happen in the representation of any State in the Senate, the executive authority of such State shall issue writs of election to fill such vacancies: *Provided,* That the legislature of any State may empower the executive thereof to make temporary appointments until the people fill the vacancies by election as the legislature may direct.
>
> This amendment shall not be construed as to affect the election or term of any Senator chosen before it becomes valid as part of the Constitution.

The Seventeenth Amendment altered fundamentally the way most senators had been chosen for 124 years. Prior to its ratification, United States senators were usually selected by the legislatures of the various states, two from each state. They served for six years, with a third of the Senate up for state legislative reelection every two years. If vacancies in Senate seats arose between elections, the state legislatures typically chose a replacement to serve the remainder of the unexpired term. If a vacancy occurred at a time when a state legislature was out of session, the governor of the state was empowered to name a temporary officeholder who would serve until the legislature reconvened and could choose a new senator.[1]

Considered by itself, the Seventeenth Amendment seemed reasonable enough—which is why it was ratified in near-record time. If democracy in limited doses is good, so went the Progressive cant at the time, more democracy could only be proportionally better. If choosing congressmen and congresswomen in the House of Representatives by popular vote works so well, then why not choose senators by direct popular elections? The fact that the Framers established a different method for choosing senators, and considered that method critical to the proper functioning of the federal government, was of no consequence.

However, the Framers did, in fact, value democratic expression. For most of them, popular democracy was a vital aspect of consensual government. But they also understood that along with its benefits there were shortcomings, and the will of the people—subject to majoritarian and factional swings and lurches—should be balanced with dispassionate, considered judgment through a stable and diffused governing construct.

The simple, logical elegance of the organization of the Senate belied the extent and passion of the discussions over its creation, both at the Constitutional Convention in Philadelphia in 1787 and in the state ratification conventions. Like nearly every clause in the Constitution, the Framers intended that the nature and operation of the Senate serve several functions simultaneously. Providing the state governments with direct input in the national government was not only an essential check on the new federal government's power, but also a means by which the states could influence congressional lawmaking, without stripping the federal government of its enumerated primacy over certain matters of governance. Moreover, the equal representation in the Senate provided the less populated states with a critical limit on the possibility that the more populated states would hold powerful sway over the affairs of the nation. In addition, the small size and relative stability of the Senate created an institutional means for tempering fleeting majoritarian or factional passions. There was also strong sentiment among the convention delegates that the Senate, by virtue of its limited size and exclusive membership, could serve as a de facto privy council for the president.

At the outset of the Constitutional Convention, Virginia governor Edmund Randolph rose to offer what would become known as the Virginia Plan for the organization of the new national government, as a point from which to begin deliberations. The plan, authored primarily by James Madison, included a bicameral national legislature, a unitary executive, and a national judiciary. The first and largest body of Congress, which would become the House of Representatives, was to be elected directly by the people. The second body, which would become the Senate, would be much smaller and chosen by the first group of candidates put forth by the state legislatures. While no specific terms of office were proposed in the Virginia Plan, it was largely understood that the members of the smaller "upper" house (Senate) would serve longer than their counterparts in the lower house (House of Representatives).[2]

The initial discussions on the Virginia Plan presented an interesting dichotomy of perspectives on the roles of the two houses of the national legislature. Madison argued strenuously for the election of the House by the people: "Mr. Madison considered the popular election of one branch of the National Legislature as essential to every plan of free Government"[3] and for "refining the popular appoints by successive filtrations . . . to be resorted to only in the appointment of the second branch of the Legislature, and in the Executive & Judiciary branches of the Government."[4]

Elbridge Gerry, a delegate from Massachusetts and future vice president of the United States, "did not like the election by the people. . . . Experience had shown that the State legislatures drawn immediately from the people did not always possess their confidence. He had no objection however to an election by the people if it were so qualified that men of honor & character might not be unwilling to be joined in the appointments. He seemed to think the people might nominate a certain number out of which the State legislatures should be bound to choose."[5] In the convention's first vote on the election of the larger house of Congress by the people, the vote was six states voting yes, two voting no, with two divided.[6]

The convention then addressed the resolution in the Virginia Plan, calling for the election by the second house of the national legislature (the Senate) by the first (the House). Richard Spaight, a delegate from North Carolina, moved to amend the resolution to say that the second branch be chosen by the state legislatures.[7] South Carolina delegate Pierce Butler "apprehended that the taking so many powers out of the hands of the States as was proposed, tended to destroy all that balance and security of interests among the States which is necessary to preserve; and called on Mr. Randolph the mover of the propositions, to explain the extent of his ideas, and particularly the number of members he meant to assign to the second branch."[8]

Randolph stated that, while he had not had in mind a specific number, "it ought to be much smaller than that of the first; so small as to be exempt from the passionate proceedings to which numerous assemblies are liable. He observed that the general object was to provide a cure for the evils under which the U.S. labored; that in tracing these evils to their origin every man had found in the turbulence and follies of democracy: that some check therefore was to be sought for against this tendency of our Governments: and that a good Senate seemed most likely to answer the purpose."[9]

Similar expressions arose throughout the convention whenever discussion of the provenance of the Senate took place. On June 7, Delaware's John Dickinson made a motion that the second house of the national legislature (the Senate) be chosen by the state legislatures. He did so because "this mode will more intimately connect the State governments with the national legislature—it will also draw forth the first characters either as to family or talent, and that it ought to consist of a considerable number."[10]

Dickinson related the upper house (Senate) to the British houses of commons and lords, "whose powers flow from different sources, are mutual checks on each other, and will thus promote the real happiness and security of the country—a government thus established would harmonize the whole."[11]

Elbridge Gerry, a skeptic throughout the convention (and, incidentally, one of only three delegates who stayed to the end and refused to sign the final Constitution), added that "the great mercantile interest and of stockholders, is not provided for in any mode of election—they will however be better represented if the State legislatures choose the second branch."[12]

George Mason of Virginia, an inveterate populist, changed his thinking and supported the motion. "Mr. Mason then spoke to the general question—observing on the propriety, that the second branch of the national legislature should flow from the legislature of each State, to prevent encroachments on each other and to harmonize the whole."[13]

Rufus King of Massachusetts made his own notes of the early debate about the means by which senators should be chosen. On the motion that there should be a large number of senators to ensure representation in the body of as many of the leading families and interests in the country as possible, King quoted Madison as saying, "The Senate should come from, and represent, the wealth of the Nation, and this being the Principle, the proposed amendment cannot be adopted.—besides the numbers will be too large—History proves this proposition, that delegated power has most weight and consequence in the hands of a few. The Roman tribunes when few, checked the Senate—when numerous, they divided, became weak and ceased to be the Guardians of the People, which was the object of their institution."[14]

Pennsylvania's James Wilson also proffered his views on a national legislative body elected by the more numerous, popularly elected House or by the state legislatures. "I well know that all confederations have been destroyed by the growth and ambition of some of their Members, and if the State Legislatures appoint the Senators, the Principle will be received by which the ancient Confederacies were ruined. I therefore propose that the Senators be elected by the People, and for this purpose, that the territory be formed into convenient divisions or Districts."[15]

Opposition to Wilson's motion was nearly unanimous. Only his own state, Pennsylvania, approved of his plan. The other states voted no. Mason, again, aptly crystallized the emphatic attitude of the convention in its consideration of the provenance of the Senate. "It is true that the old Confederacies were ruined by great overgrown power and the ambition of some of their Members—but their circumstances differed from ours—*we have agreed that the national Government shall have a negative on the acts of the State Legislatures.*—the danger now is that the national Legislature will swallow up the Legislatures of the States. The Protection from the Occurrence will be the securing to the State Legislatures, the choice of the Senators of the U.S. *So adopted unanimously.*"[16]

After the convention's draft constitution was dispatched to the states for ratification, the character of the Senate was an imperative selling point about the federal nature of the proposed national government. In *Federalist* 39, Madison went to great pains to delineate the ways in which the Constitution established a *federal, republican* form of government. "The first question that offers itself is whether the general form and aspect of the government be strictly republican. It is evident that no other form would be reconcilable with the genius of the people of America; with the fundamental principles of the Revolution; or with that honorable determination which animates every votary of freedom to rest all our political experiments on the capacity of mankind for self-government."[17]

After noting that the people of the country are, directly, the source of authority for the new federal government—hence, the "We the People" start to the preamble to the Constitution—and that the states, as independent sovereigns of governance with their own writs from the people, had to ratify the Constitution before it could take effect, Madison then dissected the proposed government to identify the *national* and *federal* aspects of its composition. While the House, elected directly by the people in proportion to the populations of the various states, was a *national* body, "[t]he Senate, on the other hand, will derive its powers from the States as political and coequal societies; and these will be represented on the principle of equality in the Senate, as they now are in the existing Congress." This circumstance, he contended, was distinctive to a *federal* government rather than a unitary *national* entity.[18]

The disposition at the state conventions was largely in favor of the Senate serving as an indispensable venue for the representation of state interests at the national level. However, other questions about the operation of the Senate arose. The Massachusetts Ratification Convention saw prolonged and passionate discussions about both the two-year term for members of the House and the six-year term for senators.[19]

The organization of the Senate was the subject of Federalist Fisher Ames's speech to the Massachusetts Ratification Convention. Ames, a highly regarded figure, said that the Senate, by its unique nature, exemplified the "sovereignty of the states," while the House of Representatives was the dominion of the "individuals." This meant that the Senate served as a "federal feature" and a guard against the national government eventually subsuming the states—a recurring complaint among delegates to the commonwealth's ratification convention. Ames even warned that if members of the Senate were elected directly by the people it would make it much easier for the federal government to "consolidate" the state governments under its control. State governments, Ames said, spoke for "the wishes and feelings and local interests of the people." They were "the safe guard and ornament of the constitution, a shelter against the abuse of power and the natural avengers of our violated rights." He characterized senators as "the ambassadors of the states."[20]

At the Virginia Ratification Convention, in response to Patrick Henry's concerns about an omnipotent federal government, Madison argued, in part, that "[t]he members to the national House of Representatives are to be chosen by the people at large, in proportion to the numbers in the respective districts. When we come to the Senate, its members are elected by the states in their equal and political capacity. But had the government been completely consolidated, the Senate would have been chosen by the people in their individual capacity, in the same manner as the members of the other house. Thus it is of a complicated nature; and this complication, I trust, will be found to exclude the evils of absolute consolidation, as well as of a mere confederacy. If Virginia was separated from all the states, her power and authority would extend to all cases: in like manner, were all powers vested in the general government, it would be a consolidated government; but the powers of the federal government are enumerated; it can only operate in certain cases; it has legislative powers on defined and limited objects, beyond which it cannot extend its jurisdiction. . . ."[21]

The only real question raised during the state ratification conventions was unrelated to the structure of the Senate. Discussions emerged over whether state legislatures could instruct senators how to vote on any given issue. The idea was even raised later in the First Congress, when the House was debating the proposal that would become the First Amendment. A congressman from South Carolina asked why the amendment did not include language providing for the right of citizens to make binding instructions to their representatives in Congress. Madison, a representative from Virginia and the lead author of the proposed amendments, said that it was redundant to do so; citizens inherently had the right to influence their representatives and state legislatures had the right to instruct their senators. It would also be impossible, as supporters of the right to instruct had wanted, to institute a penalty for senators who failed to follow explicit instructions, or for states not to be bound by federal legislation for which their edicts were ignored by their senators. This idea died when it was pointed out it would amount to a de facto veto by states of federal laws.[22]

Although there were various points of trepidation in every state ratification convention about some aspect of the Constitution's design, which were aired fully and passionately, none of the amendments to the Constitution suggested by any of the state ratification conventions included the direct popular election of senators. There were unquestionably many people from all stations in life, from every corner of the new country, represented at the state ratification conventions. Many were fearful that the new federal government would seize state authority and centralize power. The state legislatures' role in selecting senators was considered one of the most significant firewalls. There was never serious consideration of the direct popular election of both houses of Congress.

The first proposed constitutional amendment to change the way senators were chosen was introduced by Representative Henry R. Storrs, from New York, in 1826. It went nowhere. Similar amendments were introduced in 1829 and 1855, neither of which was any more successful than the first attempt. In 1868, President Andrew Johnson sent to the Senate a proposed constitutional amendment that included a provision for the popular election of senators as well as language to change the presidency to a single six-year term. That proposal died quickly.[23]

The proposal that eventually became the Seventeenth Amendment, providing for the direct popular election of senators, probably would not have become part of the Constitution had it been brought forward in other times. In fact, it failed when it was introduced several times over the decades before it was finally ratified. The idea benefited from the unique political and cultural atmosphere that consumed the nation during the late nineteenth and early twentieth centuries—a Progressive populism promoting simultaneously radical egalitarianism and centralized authoritarianism. Public sentiment grew amenable to changing the method of selecting senators. State legislatures responded to these pressures by letting the public vote, in some fashion, on who they wanted as their senators. For example, in some states the legislature would nominate candidates from each party. The state legislature would then take under advisement the public's preference in choosing the senator—effectively letting the public "vote" in a "primary" election to select the finalists from whom the legislature would pick the senator. Thirty-one states offered some manner of popular voting on senators at one time or another before the Seventeenth Amendment was ratified.

Among the most persuasive arguments offered for changing the way senators were chosen was that state legislatures were occasionally in disarray over the selection of senators, unable or unwilling to find enough votes to elect a senator, which occurred during the nineteenth century. Thus, states were denied full representation in the Senate from time to time. For example, one of Delaware's Senate seats was unoccupied from March 1899 to

March 1903. Moreover, the Delaware legislature failed to select any senators from 1901 to 1903. In 1897, in Oregon, one-third of the members of the legislature refused to take their oaths of office in order to prevent their opponents from electing the next senator. The legislature was "in session" for fifty-three days without conducting a single official act, including electing a senator.[24] All told, from 1895 to 1905, state legislatures in California, Delaware, Montana, Oregon, Pennsylvania, Utah, and Washington State failed to elect senators for periods ranging from ten months to four years.[25] Even so, vacancies for lengthy periods were rare.

The day after the Seventeenth Amendment became part of the Constitution, the balance of power that had existed between the states and the federal government since the Constitution's ratification was dealt a critical blow. The long silence of the states had begun. The states no longer had a legislative venue, or any venue, to influence directly the course of the federal government. This contributed significantly to the dismantlement of the states' traditional and exclusive areas of governing responsibility. As a result, today the federal government fills whatever areas of governance and even society it chooses. State sovereignty exists mostly at the will of the federal government. The federal government's limited nature under the Constitution was transmuted into the kind of centralized power structure the Framers worked so diligently to thwart.

Yet this proposed amendment, perhaps more than the others, may be considered the most controversial and politically difficult to institute. After all, the direct popular election of senators was sold as, among other things, empowering the people against wealthy, corrupt, and connected special interests. Opponents of the Seventeenth Amendment will undoubtedly be accused of

being "antidemocracy" and favoring "politicians choosing politicians." Of course, the Statist is the architect of the current post-
constitutional environment in which governing masterminds
attack relentlessly the individual's independence and free will.
The Statist may claim to defend "democracy" but in fact he aban-
dons the electoral process when the outcomes do not advance
his agenda. He then resorts to legal and policy evasions and
contrivances, relying on government by clandestine lawmaking,
judicial overreach, and administrative fiat, all of which destroy
self-government.

Indeed, the state convention process is a response to an oppressive federal government, the potential of which was feared
by the Framers. However, it will be opposed by the Statist, for he
may pose as a democrat, but it is democratic tyranny that he fa-
vors. Moreover, the proposed amendment, along with the others,
provides recourse against the kind of centralized and ubiquitous
edifice the federal government has become. It is the state legislatures, acting together, that can buffer the individual from the
relentless trespasses of the federal government and restore constitutional republicanism.

And what of the post–Seventeenth Amendment Senate?
Rather than spending time conferring with the elected state officials who would have sent them to Washington, D.C., and representing primarily state interests in the Senate, these senators now
spend more time with, and are more beholden to, Washington
lobbyists, campaign funders, national political consultants, and
national advocacy organizations. In fact, states are often viewed
as little more than another constituency, one among hundreds,
with interests that may or may not be relevant to or comport with
a senator's political and policy ambitions.

Furthermore, state sovereignty is not a top priority for most senators because the state legislatures hold no sway over them. Therefore, situations arise where senators vote for major federal legislation over the strenuous objections of their own states. For example, more than half of all states—twenty-seven states— joined federal litigation to overturn the so-called Patient Protection and Affordable care Act, aka Obamacare, yet the law was passed in the Senate by a large majority of sixty votes.[26] In Virginia, both senators—Mark Warner and Jim Webb—voted for Obamacare, despite strong opposition from Virginia state officials. The state attorney general, Ken Cuccinelli, was among the first to bring a lawsuit.

Consequently, as a result of one election cycle in 2008, where the Democratic Party controlled all the elected parts of the federal government for a short two-year period, there was no counterweight or check on lawmaking, which a Senate whose members were elected by the state legislatures would have provided. Although in the very next election cycle, in 2010, the Republican Party won historic victories at all levels of government, including a huge victory in the House of Representatives, the Senate and president resisted all efforts to modify or repeal Obamacare.[27] Its implementation proceeded at a feverish albeit chaotic pace, as it does today. Meanwhile, the people continue to oppose Obamacare, as they have from the outset.[28]

The Seventeenth Amendment serves not the public's interest but the interests of the governing masterminds and their disciples. Its early proponents advanced it not because they championed "democracy" or the individual, but because they knew it would be one of several important mechanisms for empowering the federal government and unraveling constitutional republicanism. And they have done so, they claim, with the consent of the citizen, for the citizen can cast a vote for his senator. Of course, the federal government's utopian mission is undeterred by voting should the citizenry vote in opposition to it. The vote is easily and routinely frustrated by all the federal branches, as is self-government generally.

The proposed amendment repeals the Seventeenth Amendment, thereby reestablishing the Senate to the character intended originally by the Framers and set forth in the Constitution. As such, it returns Congress to a true bicameral institution; provides the states with direct input into federal lawmaking decisions in real time; decentralizes the influences on a senator from Washington, D.C., to the states and local communities; and encourages a more rational, reflective, and collaborative legislating process. In addition, the proposed amendment ensures that no Senate vacancy can continue beyond ninety days and that state legislatures have the authority to remove a senator for any reason.

CHAPTER FOUR

An Amendment to Establish Term Limits for Supreme Court Justices and Super-Majority Legislative Override

SECTION 1: No person may serve as Chief Justice or Associate Justice of the Supreme Court for more than a combined total of twelve years.

SECTION 2: Immediately upon ratification of this Amendment, Congress will organize the justices of the Supreme Court as equally as possible into three classes, with the justices assigned to each class in reverse seniority order, with the most senior justices in the earliest classes. The terms of office for the justices in the First Class will expire at the end of the fourth Year following the ratification of this Amendment, the terms for the justices of the Second Class will expire at the end of the eighth Year, and of the Third Class at the end of the twelfth Year, so that one-third of the justices may be chosen every fourth Year.

SECTION 3: When a vacancy occurs in the Supreme Court, the President shall nominate a new justice who, with the approval of a majority of the Senate, shall serve the remainder of the unexpired term. Justices who fill a vacancy for longer than half of an unexpired term may not be renominated to a full term.

SECTION 4: Upon three-fifths vote of the House of Representatives and the Senate, Congress may override a majority opinion rendered by the Supreme Court.

SECTION 5: The Congressional override under Section 4 is not subject to a Presidential veto and shall not be the subject of litigation or review in any Federal or State court.

SECTION 6: Upon three-fifths vote of the several state legislatures, the States may override a majority opinion rendered by the Supreme Court.

SECTION 7: The States' override under Section 6 shall not be the subject of litigation or review in any Federal or State court, or oversight or interference by Congress or the President.

SECTION 8: Congressional or State override authority under Sections 4 and 6 must be exercised no later than twenty-four months from the date of the Supreme Court rendering its majority opinion, after which date Congress and the States are prohibited from exercising the override.

THE FRAMERS OF THE Constitution anticipated many things. They were concerned about a national executive—the president—becoming a tyrant, so they created a powerful legislature and an independent judiciary to slake presidential ambitions. They worried about the momentary passions of a tempestuous time inflaming the populous and, by extension, the Congress, so they created the presidential veto, and divided legislative authority between a House of Representatives selected by the people and a Senate chosen by the state legislatures. Some of the Framers also feared a too-autonomous judiciary that would grow in power and purview and, eventually, swallow the other branches of the federal government and the states. To protect against this, they granted Congress the power to define both the size of the Supreme Court and the makeup of the federal court system below the High Court.[1] And, with only a few exceptions, they also granted Congress the power to determine the original and appellate jurisdictions of every federal court.

In addition, to ensure that both the executive and judicial branches did not become sinecures for corrupt officeholders, they granted Congress the power to impeach and remove judges and most federal officials up to and including the president in certain cases.[2] Moreover, in order to help control the scope and reach of the central government and safeguard state sovereignty, they enumerated in detail the powers and limitations of federal authority both in the Constitution itself and what would become the Bill of Rights—the first ten amendments approved by the First Congress, and ratified by the states in 1791.

Beyond freedom from undue influence, the Framers also realized that the judiciary's independence had to come with some

significant strings attached, ensuring it fit into a republican form
of government. Federal judges were expected to adjudicate "cases
and controversies" that arose under federal criminal law and civil
statutes—and exercise very little authority beyond that narrow
scope. Contrary to the opinions of some notable Supreme Court
justices and others down through the years, the reason the Framers did not specifically grant to the Supreme Court the much
broader authority to judge the constitutionality of federal laws is
that there was strong sentiment that such a function was well outside the authority of judges. This was a primary reason Congress
was granted authority to structure the courts.

In particular, on June 4, 1787, at the Constitutional Convention, the delegates took up the issue of granting the national
executive (the title of president had not yet been adopted) the
ability to "give a negative" (veto) to any act of the national legislature. Some delegates, including James Madison, initially favored
a "council of revision" made up of the executive and judiciary,
which could reject acts of the legislature. The convention quickly
rejected the idea of including the judiciary in such a review process. They did not want judges involved in the legislative process,
thereby reviewing laws they might eventually have to adjudicate.
Instead, the delegates came up with the presidential veto.[3]

Subsequent debate centered on the size of the majorities in
the branches of the legislature necessary to override a veto, and
whether to even include the possibility of the legislature over-
riding a veto at all. Alexander Hamilton thought the executive
should be given an absolute negative over legislative acts. Pennsylvania's James Wilson observed that the mere presence of an
executive veto would cause it to be seldom used, even with a legislative override option. "The Legislature would know that such

a power existed, and would refrain from such laws, as it would be sure to defeat. [The veto's] silent operation would therefore preserve harmony and prevent mischief."[4]

The point is that the Framers clearly intended to create intrinsic limitations on the ability of any one branch or level of government to have unanswered authority over the other. Moreover, there can be no doubt that were the conditions that exist today— with the Supreme Court involving itself in minute and endless facets of everyday life—known to the convention delegates, they would undoubtedly endorse a check on judicial authority.

In *Federalist* 78, Hamilton wrote, in part:

Whoever attentively considers the different departments of power must perceive, that, in a government in which they are separated from each other, the judiciary, from the nature of its functions, will always be the least dangerous to the political rights of the Constitution; because it will be least in a capacity to annoy or injure them. The Executive not only dispenses the honors, but holds the sword of the community. The legislature not only commands the purse, but prescribes the rules by which the duties and rights of every citizen are to be regulated. The judiciary, on the contrary, has no influence over either the sword or the purse; no direction either of the strength or of the wealth of the society; and can take no active resolution whatever. It may truly be said to have neither FORCE nor WILL, but merely judgment; and must ultimately depend upon the aid of the executive arm even for the efficacy of its judgments. This simple view of the matter suggests several important consequences. It proves incontestably, that the judiciary is beyond

comparison the weakest of the three departments of power;
that it can never attack with success either of the other two;
and that all possible care is requisite to enable it to defend
itself against their attacks. It equally proves, that though
individual oppression may now and then proceed from the
courts of justice, the general liberty of the people can never
be endangered from that quarter; I mean so long as the judiciary remains truly distinct from both the legislature and
the Executive. . . .[5]

In *Anti-Federalist* 11, Brutus, believed to be New York judge
and Anti-Federalist Robert Yates, one of the most articulate opponents of the Constitution, was alarmed. He warned:

The real effect of this system of government, will therefore
be brought home to the feelings of the people, through the
medium of the judicial power. It is, moreover, of great importance, to examine with care the nature and extent of the
judicial power, because those who are to be vested with it,
are to be placed in a situation altogether unprecedented in
a free country. They are to be rendered totally independent,
both of the people and the legislature. . . . No errors they
may commit can be corrected by any power above them, if
any such power there be, nor can they be removed from office for making ever so many erroneous adjudications. . . .[6]

In addition, Yates made this prediction in *Anti-Federalist* 15:

Perhaps nothing could have been better conceived to facilitate the abolition of the state governments than the

constitution of the judicial. They will be able to extend the
limits of the general government gradually, and by insen-
sible degrees, and to accommodate themselves to the tem-
per of the people. Their decisions on the meaning of the
constitution will commonly take place in cases which arise
between individuals, with which the public will not be generally acquainted; one adjudication will form a precedent to
the next, and this to a following one.[7]

Yates, who died in 1801, did not live to see the 1803 Supreme
Court decision in *Marbury v. Madison*. No doubt he would have
been appalled. In his decision, Chief Justice John Marshall wrote,
in part, "The judicial power of the United States is extended to
all cases arising under the constitution. Could it be the intention
of those who gave this power, to say that, in using it, the constitution should not be looked into? That a case arising under the
constitution should be decided without examining the instrument
under which it arises? This is too extravagant to be maintained."[8]
It is true Marshall wrote that the judiciary should exercise "judicial review" prudently; however, this was of little consolation. By
claiming authority not specifically granted by the Constitution,
abuses of power would certainly follow, as they have.

Although the decision has been lauded by many scholars of
all philosophical stripes, the fact is that the ruling altered and expanded the Court's limited authority to adjudicate civil disputes
and criminal complaints into a judicial oligarchy with few institutional limits on its power. And the extent to which there are
limits depends on the forbearance of the very courts that snatched
the authority in the first place. It would seem that if a Supreme
Court majority of five lawyers has the final word on constitutional

matters, then governance comes down to selecting five lawyers. This is obviously contrary to the Framers' intent. Had the Constitutional Convention conferred such authority on a handful of individuals, which it most assuredly did not, it is indeed doubtful it would have conferred life terms upon them and provided no effective recourse.

No less than Thomas Jefferson, the original author of the Declaration of Independence, was furious about the *Marbury* decision. In a letter to Abigail Adams, John Adams's wife, Jefferson wrote a year after *Marbury* was issued, "The Constitution . . . meant that its coordinate branches should be checks on each other. But the opinion which gives to the judges the right to decide what laws are constitutional and what not, not only for themselves in their own sphere of action but for the Legislature and Executive also in their spheres, would make the Judiciary a despotic branch."[9]

Jefferson's concerns with judicial power became more pronounced as he passed into old age. In 1820, he wrote William Jarvis:

[T]o consider judges as the ultimate arbiters of all constitutional questions [is] a very dangerous doctrine indeed, and one which would place us under the despotism of an oligarchy. Our judges are as honest as other men and not more so. They have with others the same passions for party, for power, and the privilege of their corps . . . and their power the more dangerous as they are in office for life and not responsible, as the other functionaries are, to the elective control. The Constitution has erected no such single tribunal, knowing that to whatever hands confided, with the corruptions of time and party, its members would become despots.

It has more wisely made all the departments co-equal and co-sovereign within themselves.[10]

Decades later, President Abraham Lincoln would have to grapple with the Supreme Court's 1856 decision in the notorious *Dred Scott v. Sandford* case, which was an abomination. The issues included whether Scott, a slave, could sue for his freedom as a longtime resident of a free territory (the territories of the Louisiana Purchase) and whether Congress's ban of slavery in those territories was constitutional. Chief Justice Roger Taney, who held that office from 1836 until his death in 1864, argued for the majority of the Court's members that Scott was not a citizen, for citizenship had been confined to the white race and, therefore, Scott had no standing to sue. Moreover, he declared that Congress did not have constitutional authority to ban slavery in those territories, for it denied slaveholders property without due process.[11] Should Taney and the Court have had the final word? The *Dred Scott* decision was a major impetus for the Civil War.

On March 4, 1861, during his first inauguration speech, Lincoln said:

I do not forget the position assumed by some that constitutional questions are to be decided by the Supreme Court, nor do I deny that such decisions must be binding in any case upon the parties to a suit as to the object of that suit, while they are also entitled to very high respect and consideration in all parallel cases by all other departments of the Government. And while it is obviously possible that such decision may be erroneous in any given case, still the evil effect following it, being limited to that particular case, with the chance that it may be overruled and never become a precedent for other cases, can better be borne than could the evils of a different practice. At the same time, the candid citizen must confess that if the policy of the Government upon vital questions affecting the whole people is to be irrevocably fixed by decisions of the Supreme Court, the instant they are made in ordinary litigation between parties in personal actions the people will have ceased to be their own rulers, having to that extent practically resigned their Government into the hands of that eminent tribunal. Nor is there in this view any assault upon the court or the judges. It is a duty from which they may not shrink to decide cases properly brought before them, and it is no fault of theirs if others seek to turn their decisions to political purposes.[12]

Less than fifty years later, Woodrow Wilson, a leader of the Progressive movement who served as the twenty-eighth president from 1913 to 1921, would take the opposite view. In fact, he endorsed flat-out judicial tyranny. In 1908, Wilson argued:

The character of the process of constitutional adaption depends first of all upon the wise or unwise choice of statesmen, but ultimately and chiefly upon the option and purpose of the courts. The chief instrumentality by which the law of the Constitution has been extended to cover the facts of national development has of course been judicial interpretations,—the decisions of the courts. The process of formal amendment of the Constitution was made so difficult by the provisions of the Constitution itself that it has seldom been feasible to use it; and the difficulty of formal amendment has undoubtedly made the courts more liberal, not to say more lax, in their interpretation than they would otherwise have been. The whole business of adaption has been theirs, and they have undertaken it with open minds, sometimes even with boldness and a touch of audacity. . . .[13]

It is worth noting that Lincoln, who insisted on judicial limits, led the effort to abolish slavery. Contrarily, Wilson, who demanded an all-powerful court, enthusiastically supported segregation.[14]

Hence, in Wilson's view, the federal judiciary was to behave as a perpetual constitutional convention—without the benefit of representation and input from the states—rewriting the Constitution as a relative handful of judges divine the merits of this or that issue, nearly always promoting the centralization and concentration of power in the federal government. Of course, the constitutional structure and amendment processes are thereby eviscerated. Yet this view has gained common acceptance and widespread adherence in legal and political circles, and the behavior is self-perpetuating, for no effective systemic mechanism has been initiated to curb or halt its imprint on the Constitution.

Indeed, a movement is and has been afoot in academia and in the courts to institutionalize within the Constitution, via the judiciary, social and economic agendas that should be left to the body politic. For example, Georgetown University law professor Robin West argues that "[w]e need . . . a progressive jurisprudence—a jurisprudence that embraces rather than resists, and then reinterprets, our liberal commitment to the 'rule of law,' the content of our individual rights, and the dream of formal equality. More inclusive interpretations—more generous reimaginings—could then undergird, and in a principled way, particular constitutional arguments. Rather than relentlessly buck, deconstruct, and vilify the seeming 'naturalness' of legal arguments based on moral premises, we ought to be providing such premises, and natural and general arguments of our own. But first we need to re-imagine."[15]

Similarly, Yale law professor Bruce Ackerman has campaigned to "interpret" the Constitution's Fourteenth Amendment to implement the so-called Second Bill of Rights, in which President Franklin Roosevelt declared that the federal government should ensure "[t]he right to a useful and remunerative job in industries or shops or farms or mines of the Nation; to earn enough to provide adequate food and clothing and recreation; of every farmer to raise and sell his products at a return which will give him and his family a decent living; of every businessman, large and small, to trade in an atmosphere of freedom from unfair competition and domination by monopolies at home and abroad; of every family to a decent home; to adequate medical care and the opportunity to achieve and enjoy good health; to adequate protection from the economic fears of old age; sickness, accident, and unemployment; to a good education."[16] Ackerman said his "aim is to redeem the lost promise of the Fourteenth Amendment's vision of national citizenship through the enactment of framework statutes and the judicial development of the meaning of 'privileges' and 'immunities' of American citizenship."[17]

For Georgetown University law professor Louis Michael Seidman, the answer to the further centralization of government is not to waste time with deceptive and deceitful interpretations of constitutional provisions by his fellow law professors, as acceptable as that might be to those who seek the fundamental transformation of America, but to abandon the Constitution outright. He states plainly what others in academia and the legal profession have promoted less forthrightly. Seidman argues, "As the nation teeters at the edge of fiscal chaos, observers are reaching the conclusion that the American system of government is broken. But almost no one blames the culprit: our insistence on obedience to the Constitution, with all its archaic, idiosyncratic and downright evil provisions. . . . If we acknowledged what should be obvious— that much constitutional language is broad enough to encompass an almost infinitely wide range of positions—we might have a very different attitude about the obligation to obey. It would become apparent that people who disagree with us about the Constitution are not violating a sacred text or our core commitments. Instead, we are all invoking a common vocabulary to express aspirations that, at the broadest level, everyone can embrace. . . ."[18]

It would seem that numerous Supreme Court justices are in essential agreement with Seidman's disdain for the Constitution. Too often they look for ways to elude the Constitution's limits in order to impose their own personal policy preferences on the parties before them and society generally. One such method has been an increasing reliance on international law to supposedly justify their rulings. For example, in 2000, Associate Justice Ruth Bader Ginsburg complained that the Court did not have the "same readiness to look beyond one's shores" as other nations. "The Supreme Court has mentioned the Universal Declaration of Human Rights a spare five times and only twice in a majority decision . . . nor does the U.S. Supreme Court note the laws or decisions of other nations with any frequency."[19] She has said that a "boldly dynamic interpretation departing radically from the original understanding" of the Constitution is sometimes necessary.[20] Indeed, Ginsburg is not particularly impressed with the Constitution, despite having taken an oath to uphold it. In February 2012, while appearing on Egypt's Al-Hayat TV shortly after the Muslim Brotherhood, among others, overthrew Egyptian president Hosni Mubarak, and advising the Egyptian people on the adoption of a new constitution, Ginsburg said, in part, that "[y]ou should certainly be aided by all the constitution-writing that has gone on since the end of World War II. I would not look to the U.S. constitution, if I were drafting a constitution in the year 2012. I might look at the constitution of South Africa. That was a deliberate attempt to have a fundamental instrument of government that embraced basic human rights, had an independent judiciary. . . . It really is, I think, a great piece of work that was done. Much more recent than the U.S. constitution— Canada has a Charter of Rights and Freedoms. It dates from 1982. You would almost certainly look at the European Convention on Human Rights. Yes, why not take advantage of what there is elsewhere in the world?"[21]

In 1988, then–associate justice John Paul Stevens referred to international standards in the case *Thompson v. Oklahoma*, respecting the execution of criminals less than sixteen years of age.[22] In 2003, Associate Justice Stephen Breyer, a proponent of consulting international law in constitutional cases, gave a speech before the American Society of International Law in which he proclaimed that the "global legal enterprise . . . is now upon us."[23] In 2003, Associate Justice Anthony Kennedy cited extensively from international law when writing the Court's decision in the *Lawrence v. Texas* sodomy case.[24] There are numerous other examples.

Former associate justice Sandra Day O'Connor was even more explicit. In 2002, she asserted in a speech that "[a]lthough international law and the law of other nations are rarely binding decision on U.S. courts, conclusions reached by other countries and by the international community should at times constitute persuasive authority in American courts." She added, "While ultimately we must bear responsibility for interpreting our own laws, there is much to learn from other distinguished jurists who have given thought to the same difficult issues that we face."[25] In 2003, O'Connor wrote, "As the American model of judicial review of legislation spreads further around the globe, I think that we Supreme Court justices will find ourselves looking more frequently to the decisions of other constitutional courts, especially other common-law courts that have struggled with the same basic constitutional questions that we have; equal protection, due process, the Rule of Law in constitutional democracies."[26] In 2004, she declared in yet another speech that "[i]nternational law is no longer a specialty. . . . It is vital if judges are to faithfully discharge their duties."[27]

Of course, foreign statutes, constitutions, and judicial decisions have no legitimate relation at all to the proper role of a Supreme Court justice. The legislative history, text, and intention of lawmakers or, respecting the Constitution, the Framers' intent, cannot be divined by inquiring into or relying on international authorities. As I wrote in *Men in Black*, "The Court has so fundamentally altered its duties, and so completely rejected the limits placed on it by the Constitution's checks and balances and enumeration of powers, that the justices are in an endless search for extra-constitutional justifications and interventions to explain their activism."[28] The Court that was given life by the Constitution cannot operate outside it. Its only rightful and lawful authority exists solely within and related to the Constitution.

James Madison put it this way: "I entirely concur in the propriety of resorting to the sense in which the Constitution was accepted and ratified by the nation. In that sense alone it is the legitimate Constitution. And if that is not the guide in expounding it, there may be no security."[29]

Reality informs us that human beings are imperfect, including the mere nine individuals who serve on the Supreme Court. The fact that they hold law degrees from prestigious schools, wear black robes, and are each referred to as "Your Honor" does not change the fallibility of their nature. Nor does the fact that from time to time the Court issues rulings with which much of society agrees or which might be considered just or even exceptional. Even monarchs have been occasionally benevolent and wise. But this does not change the essential character of authoritarianism and the general mind-set of those who would rule over citizens as subjects. In fact, history belies the notion of enlightened governing masterminds, immune from republican attitudes and values. Whatever one may think of the *Marbury* decision, it cannot be denied that today the Supreme Court's power is of the sort Wilson envisioned.

For example, the Court has issued numerous politically determinative decisions, nearly all of which promote a trajectory of expanded federal power, including the Court's own authority, in defiance of the Constitution's structure and limits. On such occasions, the justices contort the facts and the law, as they must, to reach their desired result. In the 1942 *Wickard v. Filburn* case, the Court ruled that the Interstate Commerce Clause encompasses commerce that is intrastate and, therefore, the federal government has the power to regulate endless forms of private economic activity, including the production of goods and services for one's own use or use within a state; in the 1947 *Everson v. Board of Education* decision, it declared the long-standing balance between government and religion void, and the existence of a "wall of separation" between church and state, leading to the banning of prayer, nativity scenes, and crosses, among other forms of religious expression, in the public square in states and localities across the nation; in the 1965 case *Griswold v. Connecticut*, the Court found that the Constitution's so-called penumbras and emanations prohibited states from banning the sale of contraceptives (a ban that was rarely enforced); in its 1982 decision in *Plyler v. Doe*, the Court conferred a constitutional right on millions of illegal alien children to a free public education; in the 2003 *Lawrence v. Texas* case, the Court ruled that sodomy is a constitutionally protected privacy right (such laws were already being repealed by most states); and, in the 2012 Obamacare decision, the Court ruled that a penalty is a tax (contrary to the statute's text, legislative history, the Court's precedent, and the Constitution's text) and, therefore, the federal government has the power to force individuals to purchase government-designed private health insurance policies.[30]

Of course, there are many such examples. Some among us cheer these decisions; some denounce them. But should five individuals be making these political and public policy decisions and imposing them on every corner of the nation and every part of society? Should they have the final say on such matters, as they pursue even newer and more novel paths around the Constitution in exercising judicial review? It is important to recognize that the Supreme Court's record is, at times, grievous. In addition to the *Dred Scott* decision, in which the Court perverted the Constitution to promote slavery, other notable examples include the 1896 *Plessy v. Ferguson* holding, where the Court sanctioned racial segregation in public facilities under the doctrine of separate but equal; the 1944 *Korematsu v. United States* decision, where the Court gave license to the U.S. Army's internment of tens of thousands of Japanese Americans without due process; and *Roe v. Wade*, the 1973 ruling in which the Court legalized abortion throughout the nation with no constitutional basis.[31]

Judicial review can be exercised for good and bad; it can be exercised wisely and foolishly. That is the Court's record. It is the record of every governing body in the United States. It is truly absurd that so many defend the evolutionary role of the modern Court as supreme to all other institutions of government and insist on the finality of its rulings. Barely one hundred justices have served on the Supreme Court. As few as five justices can dictate economic, cultural, criminal, and security policy for the nation. One new justice, replacing a retiring or deceased justice, can sway the Court in one direction or another. Hence, the political battles for "control of the Court" when vacancies occur.

In *Men in Black* I explained, "The biggest myth about judges is that they're somehow imbued with greater insight, wisdom, and vision than the rest of us; that for some reason God Almighty has endowed them with superior judgment about justice and fairness. But the truth is that judges are men and women with human imperfections and frailties. Some have been brilliant, principled, and moral. Others have been mentally impaired, venal, and even racist."[32]

Consider a few of the stunning personalities who have served on the Court: John Rutledge, a 1795 recess appointment as the nation's second chief justice, was considered mentally unstable; Henry Brockholst Livingston, appointed in 1806, killed a man in a duel before his appointment; Henry Baldwin, appointed in 1830, was reportedly insane; Robert C. Grier, appointed in 1846, became mentally incapacitated yet continued his duties on the Court; Nathan Clifford, appointed in 1858, suffered a stroke and became a "babbling idiot"; Stephen J. Field, appointed in 1863, gradually lost his mind; Joseph McKenna, appointed in 1897, became mentally unstable and resisted retirement; James C. McReynolds, appointed in 1914 (by Woodrow Wilson), was a notorious anti-Semite and racist; Hugo Black, appointed in 1937 (by Franklin Roosevelt), had been a member of the Ku Klux Klan and remained on the Court despite his declining mental health; William O. Douglas, appointed in 1939, allegedly sexually assaulted a flight attendant in his chambers and remained on the Court despite suffering an incapacitating stroke; Abe Fortas, appointed in 1965, continued to advise President Lyndon Johnson after his appointment and supplemented his Court salary from a foundation set up by a convicted stock swindler, and was eventually forced to resign; Thurgood Marshall, appointed in 1967, in his waning years apparently spent many hours watching television in his chambers, especially soap operas.[33]

The mechanisms the Framers put into operation relating to the judiciary were designed to achieve certain vital purposes that would, in turn, help ensure the successful operation of the federal government they established. They knew the sordid history of monarchs and bureaucracies compromising jurisprudence to serve political ambitions, and they did not want that result in the United States. They sought the independence of the judiciary to help establish and preserve the integrity of the federal judicial system and, by extension, the federal government itself.

There have been many great justices and rulings. But the power the Supreme Court exercises today is not the authority contemplated or granted by the Framers (incidentally, the same can be said of the other branches). It is not sanctioned in the Constitution. It is not consonant with republican government. Moreover, impeachment is mostly a dead letter, except in outlandish cases of criminal misbehavior. However, it is clear that the notion of judicial review has long been acquiesced to and is now ingrained in such a way as to make its uprooting imprudent if not impossible. That said, there is no reason a great society must surrender, for all time and in all cases, to a judicial oligarchy exercising supreme power over the other federal branches and the states. The Supreme Court is to be independent in its judicial deliberations but not supreme in all matters, leaving society without recourse.

The proposed amendment seeks to return the Court to its proper foundational role within a republican system of government. It does the following: 1) ends the lifetime term of justices and replaces it with a single twelve-year term of office with no possibility of renomination or a second term; 2) grants Congress the authority to overturn a Supreme Court decision by a three-fifths vote of the House and Senate; and 3) grants the states authority to overturn a Supreme Court decision if three-fifths of the state legislatures pass resolutions doing so. The justices individually and the Court generally retain their independence. The justices continue to select, hear, and decide cases without interference from Congress, the executive branch, or the states. Moreover, they serve for a term longer than any two-term president and without fear of political retribution. There is no change in the Court's core judicial functions or the independence of the Court as an institution. However, the proposed amendment provides that the final say in certain matters of overarching national significant need not be left to a mere five lawyers, allowing Congress and/or the states to act by a supermajority vote.

There are also important breakwaters to prevent potential abuse of the override processes included in the language of the proposed amendment. Whether the override of a decision originated in Congress or with the state legislatures, it would apply only to the four corners of the majority opinion of the specific Supreme Court decision. It could not be used to parse the meaning of a decision or entangle precedent. The override would simply expunge the holding of the Court. If there are conflicting rulings by lower courts within or among the different judicial circuits, these would stand as the ruling precedents on the legal and/or constitutional issues relating to the litigation in those forums. Even now the Court takes up only a small fraction of the thousands of cases appealed to it each year, leaving conflicts and issues within and between judicial circuits unresolved all the time.

Nonetheless, there are always certain cases involving significant national matters, such as the constitutionality of the Obamacare law, that require resolution. The issue, then, is how to resolve them. Under the proposed amendment, the Court is still free to take up such cases and rule on them, but Congress and/or the state legislatures will also be free to override the decision with supermajority votes. By adding the override, for the first time justices will know that their most significant majority opinions may not solely be judged by history, but by the people who must live under them, with the possible ignominy of having a ruling overridden by a supermajority of the legislative branches. The override also has the benefit of requiring a fairly substantial societal consensus in order to be successfully invoked in the first place. This is also the primary reason the proposed amendment proscribes a presidential veto of an override.

Furthermore, as explained, override attempts would be time-limited. Consequently, a party or faction out of power that suddenly wins a broad mandate cannot go back over several years and override long-settled issues. The time limit also means that issues on which the override is invoked must be genuinely problematic, and not merely pursued as a political expedient. The Supreme Court typically decides more than one hundred cases a year. And the time, financial resources, manpower, and political capital necessary to shepherd an override through to reality would require sound judgment on the selection of matters worthy of focused efforts.

Finally, in transitioning from the current life tenure of a justice to the term limit, the proposed amendment's mechanism is borrowed from Article I, Section 2 of the Constitution, and the Framers' method of putting the Senate on a cycle in which one-third of the senators are chosen every two years. After the first election in 1789, the senators were organized into three classes, with the terms of the senators in the first class expiring in two years; the terms of the senators in the second class expiring in four years; and the terms of the senators in the third class expiring in six years.

Applying this concept to the Supreme Court, the proposed amendment divides the sitting Supreme Court justices into three classes by reverse seniority, with the terms of the longest-serving justices expiring first. For example, if the proposed amendment applied today, the first class would consist of Associate Justices Antonin Scalia, Anthony Kennedy, and Clarence Thomas, whose terms would expire in four years. The second class would consist of Associate Justices Ruth Bader Ginsburg and Stephen Breyer and Chief Justice John Roberts, whose terms would expire in eight years. And the third class would consist of Associate Justices Samuel Alito, Sonia Sotomayor, and Elena Kagan, whose terms would expire in twelve years.

In such a scenario, conservatives might object that three of the originalist members of the Court would be lost in the first wave of term-limited justices. A closer examination reveals more complexity. Of the three justices in the first class, Scalia and Kennedy are both seventy-seven years old. Thomas is sixty-five. By the time the state convention process would be organized by two-thirds of the states and its work completed, followed by the state ratification process—which requires approval of the amendments by a three-fourths supermajority of the states—it is highly unlikely those three justices would still be on the Court. The process underscores that this proposed amendment is not about individual justices or political advantage but strengthening the republican nature of our government.

James Madison and his fellow Convention delegates wisely settled on an independent judiciary, but they were troubled about the prospect of a supreme judiciary. As Madison later wrote, "As the courts are generally the last in making the decision, it results to them, by refusing or not refusing to execute a law, to stamp it with its final character. This makes the Judiciary department paramount in fact to the Legislature, which was never intended, and can never be proper."[34] The proposed amendment seeks to address what, in fact, has come to be.

CHAPTER FIVE

TWO AMENDMENTS TO LIMIT FEDERAL SPENDING AND TAXING

SPENDING

SECTION 1: Congress shall adopt a preliminary fiscal year budget no later than the first Monday in May for the following fiscal year, and submit said budget to the President for consideration.

SECTION 2: Shall Congress fail to adopt a final fiscal year budget prior to the start of each fiscal year, which shall commence on October 1 of each year, and shall the President fail to sign said budget into law, an automatic, across-the-board, 5 percent reduction in expenditures from the prior year's fiscal budget shall be imposed for the fiscal year in which a budget has not been adopted.

SECTION 3: Total outlays of the United States Government for any fiscal year shall not exceed its receipts for that fiscal year.

SECTION 4: Total outlays of the United States Government for each fiscal year shall not exceed 17.5 percent of the Nation's gross domestic product for the previous calendar year.

SECTION 5: Total receipts shall include all receipts of the United States Government but shall not include those derived from borrowing. Total outlays shall include all outlays of the United States Government except those for the repayment of debt principal.

SECTION 6: Congress may provide for a one-year suspension of one or more of the preceding sections in this Article by a three-fifths vote of both Houses of Congress, provided the vote is conducted by roll call and sets forth the specific excess of outlays over receipts or outlays over 17.5 percent of the Nation's gross domestic product.

SECTION 7: The limit on the debt of the United States held by the public shall not be increased unless three-fifths of both Houses of Congress shall provide for such an increase by roll call vote.

SECTION 8: This Amendment shall take effect in the fourth fiscal year after its ratification.

TAXING

SECTION 1: Congress shall not collect more than 15 percent of a person's annual income, from whatever source derived. "Person" shall include natural and legal persons.

SECTION 2: The deadline for filing federal income tax returns shall be the day before the date set for elections to federal office.

SECTION 3: Congress shall not collect tax on a decedent's estate.

SECTION 4: Congress shall not institute a value-added tax or national sales tax or any other tax in kind or form.

SECTION 5: This Amendment shall take effect in the fourth fiscal year after its ratification.

The nation is teetering on financial ruin due to the unconscionable profligate spending, borrowing, taxing, and money printing by the federal government. Several decades ago, Dr. Milton Friedman, an iconic economist and Nobel laureate, concluded that "it is not in the interest of a legislator to vote against a particular appropriation bill if that vote would create strong enemies while a vote in its favor would alienate few supporters. That is why simply electing the right people is not a solution."[1] The solution is to remove by constitutional design that which cannot be accomplished statutorily—the overwhelming political incentive for reckless government spending by the governing masterminds.

For more than four years, since April 29, 2009, Congress and the president have refused to adopt a budget. Both branches were in violation of the Congressional Budget and Impoundment Control Act of 1974 (Budget Act).[2] And during this period and since, the federal government has unleashed a spending blitz unparalleled in American history.

The Budget Act sets forth a budgeting process requiring the president to propose a budget in February; Congress to adopt an annual budget resolution setting forth its budget blueprint; Congress to subsequently pass a budget resolution laying out timetables for completing a final budget; and a final budget, which the president either signs or vetoes.[3] However, from fiscal year 2010 through the early part of 2013 Congress passed seventeen continuing resolutions, which are stopgap funding measures, because the Senate refused to comply with the Budget Act's requirements.

In addition to short-term spending bills, Congress has also legislated by adopting massive omnibus bills that even voting members cannot comprehend. For example, in 1989, Congress passed a budget reconciliation act that one prominent member of Congress described as follows: "So voluminous was this monster bill that it was hauled into the chamber in an oversized box. Its thousands of pages, which the clerk hadn't even time to number, had to be tied together with rope, like newspapers bundled for recycling. While reading it was obviously out of the question, it's true that I was permitted to walk around the box and gaze upon it from several angles, and even to touch it."[4]

Rather than enforcing budgetary and spending discipline, Congress and the president have raised the debt limit eleven times between 2001 and 2012, increasing massively the federal debt by trillions of dollars.[5]

Clearly, Congress and the president knowingly subvert their own legal budgetary requirements for the purpose of increasing spending while attempting to mask political responsibility from the public. They are dragging the nation into a financial death spiral. Their opportunism and dysfunction threaten a financial implosion that presages the eventual collapse of the nation's currency and economy, resulting in unimaginable devastation and misery. Therefore, restraint must be imposed on a broken federal system by constitutional amendment and, if possible, promptly.

Four years following ratification of the proposed Spending Amendment, Congress must adopt a final, annual fiscal year budget prior to the start of each fiscal year; keep spending at or under 17.5 percent of the gross domestic product (GDP) each fiscal year, requiring Congress and the executive branch to prioritize appropriations; and balance the federal budget each fiscal year (with a proviso for emergencies), thereby starting to limit the hemorrhaging of spending and debt accumulation passed from one generation to the next.

As the facts make undeniable, the nation is running out of time. Federal fiscal spending in real dollars has increased to unsustainable levels. For *fiscal operations* alone, in 2002, the federal government spent a little over $2 trillion. By 2008, it spent $2.98 trillion. In 2009, federal spending increased to $3.5 trillion. For 2010 and 2011, federal spending was $3.45 and $3.6 trillion, respectively. In 2012, federal spending was $3.79 trillion.[6]

As a percentage of GDP, federal spending for fiscal operations is historically sky-high. In 2002, federal outlays as a percentage of GDP were 19.1 percent. By 2008, outlays increased to 20.8 percent. In 2009, they increased to 25.2 percent. For 2010 and 2011, spending as a percentage of GDP was 24.1 percent, respectively. In 2012, outlays accounted for 24.3 percent of GDP.[7]

Federal deficits for annual fiscal operations have increased astronomically. In 2002, the federal government incurred a budget deficit of $157 billion. In other words, spending on current governmental operations for the year exceeded receipts by $157 billion. By 2008, the budget deficit increased to $458 billion. In 2009, it jumped to a staggeringly high $1.4 trillion. In 2010 and 2011, it reached $1.29 trillion for each year ($2.58 trillion total). For 2012, the federal deficit was $1.32 trillion.[8]

In May 2013, the Congressional Budget Office (CBO) released information widely touted as good news. The fiscal operating deficit was estimated to be $642 billion, $200 billion less than the CBO had originally projected and 4 percent of GDP. But Keith Hennessey, former director of the U.S. National Economic Council, explained, "Any time you hear a deficit number, compare it to zero, two, and three, and you'll have a good feel for where we are. A 4 percent deficit for this year is not good; it's almost twice as high as the historic average, and it's high enough that our debt will continue to increase faster than our economy will grow."[9]

In contrast, while some state governments are horribly managed, many require the enactment of yearly balanced budgets. In 2008, it was reported that governors in forty-four states are required to submit balanced budgets, of which thirty-four are mandated by state constitutions and ten by state statutes. Forty-one states require their legislatures to pass annual balanced budgets, of which thirty-three are compelled by state constitutions and the remaining eight by state statutes.[10]

However, with increases in yearly federal deficits come increases in the *overall federal debt*. The total federal debt resulting solely from spending on fiscal operations as a percentage of GDP has increased dramatically since 2002. In 2002, this debt as a percentage of GDP was 58.8 percent. By 2008, it rose to 69.7 percent. In 2009, it jumped to 85.2 percent. In 2010 and 2011, debt as a percentage of GDP was 94.2 percent and 98.7 percent, respectively. For 2012, federal debt was 104.8 percent of GDP.[11] Consequently, the federal debt is now larger than the entire annual value of all the goods and services produced by the nation's private sector.

The federal debt in real dollar amounts for fiscal operations has also reached staggering heights. For 2008, the figure was $10.69 trillion; $12.14 trillion in 2009; $13.8 trillion in 2010; $15.22 trillion in 2011; and more than $16.3 trillion in 2012. The federal debt for fiscal operations under the Obama administration has increased almost $6 trillion.[12] In 2012, as a result of this massive debt, every taxpayer was on the hook for $111,000, while the average income was about $51,000. And by 2022, the debt from fiscal operating expenses is estimated to exceed $25 trillion.[13]

Simply making the enormous interest payments on this debt will become overwhelming. "CBO projects that the government's yearly net interest spending will more than triple between 2011 and 2021 (from $225 billion to $792 billion) and double as a share of GDP (from 1.5 percent to 3.3 percent)." According to the CBO, "large budget deficits and growing debt would reduce national savings, leading to higher interest rates, more borrowing from abroad, and less domestic investment—which in turn would lower the growth of incomes in the United States."[14]

None of this takes into consideration the total *unfunded liability* of major entitlement programs, which is absolutely ruinous. The total unfunded liability of Medicare as of 2012 was $42.8 trillion. The program's trustees concluded that Medicare spending could consume roughly 10.4 percent of GDP in 2086. "Growth of this magnitude, if realized, would substantially increase the strain on the nation's workers, the economy, Medicare beneficiaries, and the federal budget."[15]

The total unfunded liability of Social Security as of 2012 was $20.5 trillion. The program's trustees concluded that "[b]eginning in 2021, annual costs exceed total income, and therefore assets begin to decline . . . at the beginning of 2022."[16]

Therefore, total obligations by the federal government—that is, *the accumulated debt from yearly fiscal operations plus the net present value of all unfunded liabilities*—amounted to over $90 trillion in 2012. Moreover, the real yearly deficits, adding together all debt and liabilities, in 2011 and 2012 were about $4.6 trillion and $6.9 trillion, respectively![17]

Consequently, for the first time in the nation's history, the federal government's credit rating has been downgraded. On August 5, 2011, citing a "negative long-term outlook," the credit rating agency Standard & Poor's downgraded the credit rating of the United States government from the highest AAA rating to AA+. It could be lowered again to AA if the rating agency sees "less reduction in spending than agreed to, higher interest rates, or new fiscal pressures during the period [resulting] in a higher general government debt trajectory."[18] On June 8, 2012, Standard & Poor's affirmed this gloomy outlook, stating, "The negative outlook reflects our opinion that U.S. sovereign credit risks, primarily political and fiscal, could build to the point of leading us to lower our AA+ long-term rating by 2014."[19]

In 2012, the Government Accountability Office (GAO) issued its own warning. Having conducted a number of reviews of the federal government's fiscal condition, it reported that the "GAO's simulations continue to illustrate that the federal government is on an unsustainable long-term fiscal path. In both the Baseline Extended and Alternative simulations, debt held by the public grows as a share of gross domestic product (GDP) over the long term. While the timing and pace of growth varies depending on the assumptions used, neither set of assumptions achieves a sustainable path. . . ."[20] In other words, the nation is facing eventual economic collapse.

In response to these disastrous fiscal and financial policies, the Federal Reserve System (Fed) has aggressively pursued monetary policies that are equally ruinous. When the Fed was established in 1913, its original mission was to ensure a stable monetary system and sound dollar. Today the Fed's authority extends to "conduct the nation's monetary policy by influencing money and credit conditions in the economy in pursuit of full employment and stable prices; supervise and regulate banks and other important financial institutions to ensure the safety and soundness of the nation's banking and financial system and to protect the credit rights of consumers; maintain the stability of the financial system and contain systemic risk that may arise in financial markets; provide certain financial services to the U.S. government, U.S. financial institutions, and foreign official institutions, and play a major role in operating and overseeing the nation's payments systems."[21] This is vast power in the hands of a relatively few governing masterminds—seven members of the board of governors and five of the twelve Federal Reserve Bank presidents composing the Federal Open Market Committee. They meet every six weeks to vote on monetary policy.

As such, with virtually unencumbered power to manipulate markets, over the last several years the Fed has launched a controversial quantitative easing campaign in which it has monetized trillions of dollars in debt—that is, the Fed creates credit, which is essentially the same as printing money, and uses it to buy federal government bonds, such as Treasury notes and mortgage-backed securities, thereby piling debt upon debt and pumping money into the economy.

The Fed has also held interest rates at historically low levels for years, thereby distorting market behavior and setting the stage for further economic destabilization as interest rates eventually rise—as they must.

In addition, the Fed has stated that it will devalue the dollar by 33 percent over the next twenty years, which will cut the dollar's value by one-third and drive up prices and costs while reducing the value of savings and investments.[22]

Further troubling is the Fed's use of what is dubbed "financial repression," where private banks are both forced and encouraged, through loosened capital and other regulatory requirements, to buy ever more government debt. As larger and larger bank holdings consist of this debt, it could eventually set off a financial time bomb, should the government renege on its obligations.[23]

Therefore, rather than ameliorating the consequences of out-of-control fiscal policies, born of political ideology and expediency, the Fed's monetary manipulations and interventions are facilitating economic chaos, which can easily lead to hyperinflation and the devaluation of the currency, including sky-high prices and the destruction of wealth; stagflation, including sky-high prices and significant economic contraction; or even deflation and the collapse of prices for goods and services.

It is obvious that few institutions are unaffected by the reckless fiscal policies of the federal government, including the Fed's reactionary role respecting its monetary responsibilities, which makes imperative the need to impose constitutional limits on the federal government's spending power. The federal government's fiscal situation is disastrous and dire, resulting from its boundless intervention in and manipulation of the individual and his environment. The evidence is unequivocal and overwhelming.

In *Democracy in America*, Alexis de Tocqueville warned that ceaseless intervention was a risk for America resulting from the nature of democracy: "In democratic societies . . . there exists an urge to do something even when the goal is not precise, a sort of permanent fever that turns to innovation of every kind. And innovations are almost always costly." [24]

The proposed Tax Amendment's ceiling on income taxes operates in concert with the spending limitations. It is intended to impose rational decision-making on Congress by strengthening the link between spending and taxing within our constitutional construct. Capping the income tax will establish a workable, stable, and predictable taxing environment, which encourages enterprise and economic growth. Moreover, the proposed amendment prevents resort to alternative forms of taxation, such as the value-added tax (VAT), for the objective is to shrink the federal Leviathan and fund only the legitimate and limited functions of the federal government.

It is worth remembering that the Framers debated with great force the federal government's size and authority. Many predicted that the federal government's taxing authority, combined with its power to provide for the "general welfare," might lead eventually to an unbridled, all-powerful national government, dominating the states and the individual. In one of many examples where the Anti-Federalists raised prescient concerns, Robert Yates, aka Brutus, wrote:

> It is as absurd to say, that the power of Congress is limited to these general expressions, "to provide for the common safety, and general welfare," as it would be to say, that it would be limited, had the constitution said they should have power to lay taxes, etc, at will and pleasure. Were this authority given, it might be said, that under it the legislature could not do injustice, or pursue any measures, but such as were calculated to promote the public good, and happiness.[25]

Yates argued earlier that "[t]he powers of the general legislature extend to every case that is of the least importance—there is nothing valuable to human nature, nothing dear to freemen, but what is within its power. It has authority to make laws which will affect the lives, the liberty, and property of every man in the United States. . . ."[26] He insisted that the limits placed on Congress's taxing power were insufficient:

> [T]he legislature [has] authority to contract debts at [its] discretion; [it is] the sole [judge] of what is necessary to provide

for the common defence, and [it] only [is] to determine what is for the general welfare; this power therefore is neither more nor less, than a power to lay and collect taxes, imposts, and excises, at [its] pleasure; not only the power to lay taxes unlimited, as to the amount [it] may require, but it is perfect and absolute to raise them in any mode [it] please[s].[27]

However, in *Federalist* 41, James Madison dismissed the critics. He noted that some Anti-Federalists had asserted that the taxing power "amount[ed] to an unlimited commission to exercise every power which may be alleged to be necessary for the common defense or general welfare." But Madison declared that "the idea of an enumeration of particulars which neither explain nor qualify the general meaning, and can have no other effect than to confound and mislead, is an absurdity. . . ."[28]

Thomas Jefferson, who had not attended the Constitutional Convention but had followed closely its deliberations, resisted the objections as well. He argued that the power to lay taxes to provide for the general welfare was not viewed by the Framers as all-encompassing: "For the laying of taxes is the power, and the general welfare the purpose, for which the power is to be exercised. Congress are [sic] not to lay taxes *ad libitum*, for any purpose they please; but only to pay the debts, or provide for the general welfare of the Union." Jefferson understood that allowing Congress to levy taxes for any purpose would essentially be a grant of a "distinct and independent power to do any act [Congress] pleased." Such a grant of power "would reduce the [Constitution] to a single phrase, that of instituting a congress with power to do whatever would be for the good of the United States; and, as they would be the sole judges of the good or evil, it would also be a power to do whatever evil they pleased." [29] Jefferson was certainly not alone in this view.

Nonetheless, led by the Massachusetts Ratification Convention in early 1788, several states warned that should the Constitution be ratified, the new Congress needed to place further limits on the grant of federal taxing authority.

Amos Singletary, a grist mill operator, father of nine, and local justice of the peace with no formal education, spoke for many during the Massachusetts Ratification Convention:

> We contended with Great Britain—some said for a three-penny duty on tea, but it was not that—it was because they claimed a right to tax us and bind us in all cases whatever. And does not this Constitution do the same? Does it not take away all we have—all our property? Does it not lay *all* taxes, duties, imposts and excises? And what more have we to give? They tell us Congress won't lay dry taxes upon us, but collect all the money they want by impost. I say there has always been a difficulty about impost [raising enough funds] . . . they will not be able to raise money enough by impost and then they will lay it on the land, and take all we have got. These lawyers and men of learning, and monied men, that talk so finely and gloss over matters so smoothly, to make us poor illiterate people swallow down the pill, except to get into Congress themselves; they expect to be the managers of the constitution and get all the power and all the money into their own hands, and then they will swallow up all us little folks like the great *Leviathan*, Mr. President, yes, just as the whale swallowed up Jonah. [30]

The Massachusetts delegation voted for ratification, but urged that an amendment to the Constitution provide that when monies raised from impost and excise taxes were insufficient for the national government's purposes, Congress would requisition additional funds from the states to raise as they deemed fit. Only if a state failed or refused to pay a requisitioned amount could Congress levy a tax on the state directly.[31] The Virginia and Rhode Island ratification conventions followed Massachusetts's lead.[32] In the end, however, no change was made to the Constitution, for the enumerations setting forth the limited grant of power to Congress were believed by the state ratification conventions as both obvious and sufficient.

In the 1830s, Supreme Court associate justice Joseph Story, considered one of the greatest legal minds of his time, emphasized the limits on the Constitution's taxation authority:

> [Jefferson's] opinion [on Congress's limited power to tax and appropriate] has been maintained at different and distant times by many eminent statesmen. It was avowed, and apparently acquiesced in, in the state conventions, called to ratify the constitution and it has been on various occasions, adopted by congress, and may fairly be deemed, that which the deliberate sense of a majority of the nation has at all times supported.[33]

Story's own view was that the specific language of the taxation clause, in which Congress may "lay and collect taxes, duties, imposts, and excises, to pay the debts and provide for the common defense, and general welfare of the United States," was indeed limiting. For Story, it was obvious that the drafters intended the power to tax to apply to only three purposes: "to pay the debts," "to provide for the common defense," and to provide for the "general welfare of the United States." The power to tax is strictly tied to these three purposes. It is not a general, unlimited power, granting Congress plenary authority, contrary to the specific enumeration of powers in Article I, the explicit recognition of individual and state sovereignty in the Bill of Rights, and the matrix of checks and balances built into the Constitution. No one believes the Framers intended to create, as Story explained, "an unlimited national government."[34]

Story underscored the importance of placing limits on federal power to levy and collect taxes:

> A power to lay taxes for any purposes whatsoever is a general power; a power to lay taxes for certain specified purposes is a limited power. A power to lay taxes for the common defence and general welfare of the United States is not in common sense a general power. It is limited to those objects. It cannot constitutionally transcend them. If the defence proposed by a tax be not the common defence of the United States, if the welfare be not general, but special, or local, as contradistinguished from national, it is not within the scope of the constitution.[35]

This should, once and for all, put to the rest the notion that by "general welfare" the Framers intended to grant Congress "general power" to tax. The Federalists insisted the Constitution effectively limited the taxing authority whereas the Anti-Federalists were concerned that the language would be distorted by future Congresses. There was overwhelming concurrence that

Congress should not be, and was not, granted plenary taxing power.

For the first few decades of the nation's history, it appeared that Madison and the other delegates were correct in concluding that the taxing power would be applied as intended. But over time, Congress pushed its limits. In 1861, in order to pay for the growing Civil War debt, Congress passed the Revenue Act, which included an income tax. However, it was repealed in 1872 because it was considered an emergency tax. Indeed, in writing to the chairman of the House Ways and Means Committee, the then-commissioner of internal revenue urged the tax's repeal. He argued that the income tax was "the one of all others most obnoxious to the genius of our people, being inquisitorial in its nature, and dragging into public view an exposition of the most private pecuniary affairs of the citizen."[36]

In 1894, Congress enacted a flat-rate income tax. But in 1895, in *Pollock v. Farmers' Loan & Trust Co.*, the Supreme Court ruled that the income tax was an unconstitutional direct tax. (A direct tax is a type of tax levied upon the individual directly rather than a tax levied on the purchase of a good or the importation of a good from outside the country.)[37] Under the Constitution, direct taxes must be apportioned among the states, meaning each state must pay its portion of the total tax based on that state's percentage of the general population.

However, the federal income tax—a "progressive" income tax—was a central goal of the Progressive movement. And in 1909, President William Howard Taft urged its adoption through the passage of a Sixteenth Amendment to the Constitution. It was passed quickly by Congress the same year. By 1913, three-fourths of the states ratified it. Then, as now, much of the political debate for the federal income tax was based on shifting the burden of taxation from the broader population to a much smaller segment of society.

Nonetheless, the early tax rates were relatively modest. The original federal income tax rates in 1913 were, in inflation-adjusted brackets, as follows: 1 percent for incomes up to $463,826; 2 percent for incomes between $463,826 to $1,159,566; 3 percent for incomes between $1,159,566 to $1,739,348; 4 percent for incomes between $1,739,348 to $2,319,131; 5 percent for incomes between $2,319,131 to $5,797,828; 6 percent for incomes between $5,797,828 to $11,595,657; and 7 percent for incomes over $11,595,657.[38]

Whereas the top rate in 1913 was 7 percent, which applied to very few individuals, federal income tax rates today are far more onerous. In the first place, in 2009, for which the latest numbers are available, the CBO reports that the bottom 20 percent of income earners' average rate for the individual income tax was negative 9.3 percent. For those in the 20–40 percent range of income earners, the average income tax was a little over negative 2 percent. Refundable tax credits exceeded the income tax owed by these individuals. Thus the income tax system today not only is intended to tax higher earners at higher rates, but directly subsidizes a substantial portion of the population with cash payments.[39]

In 2009, for individuals in the 40–60 percent range, the average income tax was 1.3 percent, while those in the 60–80 percent range had an average income tax rate of 4.6 percent. The top 20 percent of earners paid, on average, a 13.4 percent income tax rate, while the top 1 percent paid on average 21 percent.[40]

The Tax Foundation reports that "the federal deficit [each year] has grown so large that "[e]ven if the government took all of the income earned by those who have an after-tax income of $1 million or more, the amount of revenue generated would fall far short of eliminating" the over $1 trillion deficit each year. In 2010, for example, the after-tax income of all millionaires was about $709 billion. The 2012 fiscal operating deficit was $1.32 trillion.[41]

It follows that higher-income earners account for most of the individual income tax revenue the federal government receives. The top 1 percent (adjusted gross income [AGI] of $343,927 and above) paid 36.73 percent of federal income taxes; the top 5 percent (AGI of $154,642 and above) paid 58.66 percent; the top 10 percent (AGI of $112,124 and above) paid 70.47 percent; the top 25 percent (AGI of $66,193 and above) paid 87.3 percent; the top 50 percent (AGI of $32,396 and above) paid 97.75 percent.[42]

Put another way, the Tax Foundation explains that "the share of taxes paid by the richest 10 percent of households, the share of all market income earned by that group, and the ratio of what that 10 percent of households pays in taxes versus what they earn as a share of the nation's income, is the highest or most 'progressive' in the industrialized world."[43] In 2013, the effective tax rate for the wealthiest households will increase further as itemized deductions have been eliminated or phased out.[44]

Hence, class warfare or soaking the so-called rich may make for good populist demagoguery and serve the political ends of the governing masterminds, but it does nothing to solve the grave realities of the federal government's insatiable appetite for spending and its inability to reform itself.

The current spending trend makes certain an immense tax increase on the vast majority of income-earning Americans, despite the overall inconsequence of taxation on bringing down the

aggregate debt. There is already talk of a VAT, which is an enormous, hidden sales tax levied at every level of production and service and drives up prices to the consumer;[45] overhauling the over
$3 trillion 401(k) retirement system, including the elimination
of nearly $80 billion in deferred taxation;[46] reducing or elimi-
nating the home mortgage interest deduction;[47] and reducing or
eliminating charitable deductions.[48] While terribly destructive of
individual and private sector wealth, these taxes and others will
be meaningless and increasingly desperate gestures.

New York Times columnist and leftist economist Paul Krugman, in a moment of candor, stated:

> Eventually we do have a problem. That the population is
> getting older, health care costs are rising . . . there is this
> question of how we're going to pay for the programs. The
> year 2025, the year 2030, something is going to have to
> give . . . we're going to need more revenue. . . . Surely it will
> require some sort of middle class taxes as well. We won't
> be able to pay for the kind of government the society will
> want without some increase in taxes . . . on the middle class,
> maybe a value-added tax. And we're also going to have to
> make decisions about health care, not pay for health care
> that has no demonstrated medical benefits. So the snarky
> version, which I shouldn't even say because it will get me in
> trouble, is death panels and sales taxes is how we do this.[49]

In addition to the financial burden and economic disloca-
tion, the tax system and Internal Revenue Code have become so
complex and oppressive that the federal government's National

Taxpayer Advocate reported in 2012, "U.S. taxpayers (both individuals and businesses) [spend] more than 6.1 billion hours to complete filings required by a tax code that contains almost four million words and that, on average, has more than one new provision added to it daily. Indeed, few taxpayers complete their returns without assistance. Nearly 60 percent of taxpayers hire paid preparers and another 30 percent rely on commercial software to prepare their returns."[50] Therefore, not only is the individual's wealth diminished by confiscatory taxation applied to unconstitutional purposes, but he is tormented by the manner in which he calculates and confers his wealth to the federal government, for which fines and penalties are imposed for miscalculations.

Moreover, the recent scandal involving the widespread targeting of tea party, conservative, and religious groups for abusive if not unlawful scrutiny, the purpose of which was to deter them from pursuing tax-exempt designations and fully participating in public advocacy, is the latest in a long history of egregious manipulation and politicization of the Internal Revenue Service (IRS) by, among others, presidents, members of Congress, and partisan bureaucrats.[51]

Over time, the limitations on the taxing power contemplated by the Framers and enshrined in the Constitution have been steadily eroded. Most recently and grievously, in the Supreme Court's 5 to 4 decision on June 28, 2012, in *National Federation of Independent Business et al. v. Sebelius, Secretary of Health and Human Services, et al.* (aka the Affordable Care Act or Obamacare case), the Court issued the most unscrupulous of modern judicial rulings, in which it not only distorted the federal government's taxing power beyond all recognition, but also used that power to alter fundamentally the relationship between the individual and the federal government.[52] The majority, led by Chief Justice John Roberts, was determined to uphold Obamacare despite the law's unconstitutional mandate, which compelled individuals to engage in commerce—that is, the purchase of a government-designed private health-care policy. It seized on the Constitution's original and limited tax provision to rewrite the law. The majority ignored the legislative history, the actual text of the statute, the Court's precedent, and the Constitution's text to redefine Obamacare's penalty provision as a tax. As the dissent wrote, in part:

> Judicial tax-writing is particularly troubling. Taxes have never been popular, see, e.g., Stamp Act of 1765, and in part for that reason, the Constitution requires tax increases to originate in the House of Representatives. That is to say, they must originate in the legislative body most accountable to the people, where legislators must weigh the need for the tax against the terrible price they might pay at their next election, which is never more than two years off. The Federalist No. 58 "defend[ed] the decision to give the origination power to the House on the ground that the Chamber that is more accountable to the people should have the primary role in raising revenue." We have no doubt that Congress knew precisely what it was doing when it rejected an earlier version of this legislation that imposed a tax instead of a requirement-with-penalty. Imposing a tax through judicial legislation inverts the constitutional scheme, and places the power to tax in the branch of government least accountable to the citizenry.[53]

And on top of it all, Obamacare relies heavily on the IRS to enforce key provisions of the law. In addition to hiring thousands of new staffers, including auditors, a recent Treasury Department Inspector General report discloses that the IRS has created several committees, offices, and teams to implement and oversee Obamacare:

- The Affordable Care Act (ACA) Executive Steering Committee (ESC) is responsible for overall program coordination and implementation of the ACA across the IRS. This committee is co-chaired by the Deputy Commissioner for Services and Enforcement and the Deputy Commissioner for Operations Support. It also includes the IRS Chief of Staff and other IRS executives, including the business operating division commissioners, et al.
- Three program management offices (PMO): 1) Services and Enforcement; 2) Modernization and Information Technology Services (MITS); and 3) Health Care Council. These PMOs are accountable to the ESC for ACA implementation and work with the IRS business operating divisions to ensure efforts are successfully coordinated.
- Four functional ESCs, each led by an executive chair, have responsibility for specific provisions in the ACA that directly affect the four business operating divisions (Wage and Investment, Small Business/Self-Employed, Large Business and International, and Tax Exempt/ Government Entities).
- The Services and Enforcement Exchange Working Teams are responsible for planning the implementation of the exchange provisions scheduled for 2014.[54]

Amos Singletary's fears, among those of others, are now fully realized.

The proposed Tax Amendment would set a ceiling for income earners at 15 percent. It provides a degree of flexibility by allowing Congress to institute a flat tax lower than 15 percent or additional income-based tax rates below the 15 percent cap. Thus, individuals at lower income levels, such as those who work part-time, students with summer jobs, adults in low-skilled jobs, retired senior citizens, etc., would pay less in taxes in absolute dollars and/or be subject to lower tax rates.

The proposed Tax Amendment eliminates all forms of double taxation, including the so-called inheritance or death tax (a tax on estates often passed from parents and grandparents to their offspring); taxes on investment income (which promotes wealth creation and economic growth); and taxes on corporations (which reduce research, capital expansion, and job creation). In most cases, these taxes have been layered upon income taxes already paid by individuals.

In addition, the proposed Tax Amendment moves the deadline for filing federal income tax returns to the day before federal elections—currently from April 15 to the first Monday in November, the day before election day. Therefore, rather than an almost seven-month gap between the filing of federal income tax returns and voting on election day, which is the situation today, the voter is able to cast his ballot with the real and personal consequences of a candidate's tax and spending record or promises fresh in mind. Linking the two events of tax-paying and voting, in a way and at a time when the voter's attention is most concen-

trated, is intended to improve political and governing accountability.

Moreover, the proposed Tax and Spending Amendments,
together, will force Congress to address the growing catastrophe
of unfunded obligations, including reforming the Medicare and
Social Security programs to meet inescapable actuarial and economic realities. Finally, the current Rube Goldberg–like tax code
will be dispatched, along with much of the IRS bureaucracy, and
replaced with a relatively simple and straightforward tax collection system that no longer torments and abuses the taxpayer. The
cap on taxes will also eliminate the confiscatory and complex nature of federal taxation that exists today.[55]

The Framers' expectation that federal spending and taxes
would be limited to support only explicitly constitutional
functions—to "pay debts and provide for the common defense
and general welfare"—has been distorted deliberately as part of
the Statists' design. It is folly to believe that Congress and the
president, on their own, will make the necessary and difficult decisions to address the impending financial debacle. After all, they
and their predecessors engineered the approaching tsunami. As
the situation becomes direr, the federal government's actions will
grow more oppressive.

The proposed Spending and Tax Amendments work in con-
junction and seek to avert a societal implosion.

CHAPTER SIX

An Amendment to Limit the Federal Bureaucracy

SECTION 1: All federal departments and agencies shall expire if said departments and agencies are not individually reauthorized in stand-alone reauthorization bills every three years by a majority vote of the House of Representatives and the Senate.

SECTION 2: All Executive Branch regulations exceeding an economic burden of $100 million, as determined jointly by the Government Accountability Office and the Congressional Budget Office, shall be submitted to a permanent Joint Committee of Congress, hereafter the Congressional Delegation Oversight Committee, for review and approval prior to their implementation.

SECTION 3: The Committee shall consist of seven members of the House of Representatives, four chosen by the Speaker and three chosen by the Minority Leader; and seven members of the Senate, four chosen by the Majority Leader and three chosen by the Minority Leader. No member shall serve on the Committee beyond a single three-year term.

SECTION 4: The Committee shall vote no later than six months from the date of the submission of the regulation to the Committee. The Committee shall make no change to the regulation, either approving or disapproving the regulation by majority vote as submitted.

SECTION 5: If the Committee does not act within six months from the date of the submission of the regulation to the Committee, the regulation shall be considered disapproved and must not be implemented by the Executive Branch.

IN ELEMENTARY SCHOOL, CHILDREN are taught that the Constitution establishes a federal government composed of three branches: the legislative, executive, and judicial. Articles I, II, and III of the Constitution create and grant limited powers and defined roles to each branch. This concept, known as separation of powers, is designed to ensure that no single body becomes too powerful and thus rules tyrannically over the others, the states, and the people. The Constitution, through an arrangement of separate but coequal branches, checks and balances, enumerated powers, federalism, and a bill of rights, diffuses power. This construct was intended to prevent the overcentralization and concentration of power in the federal government and was fundamental to preserving the nature of republican government.

Article I specifically vests Congress with the legislative power.

Congress is most directly accountable to the people (the House, whose members are elected directly, and the Senate, whose members were originally chosen by the states). It stands to reason that the power to establish laws would fall to it. Article I provides, in part, "All legislative powers herein granted shall be vested in a Congress of the United States. . . ."[1] In *Federalist* 48, James Madison envisions Congress as potentially the most powerful of the three branches. He explained, "The legislative department derives a superiority in our governments from other circumstances. Its constitutional powers being at once more extensive, and less susceptible of precise limits, it can, with the greater facility, mask, under complicated and indirect measure, the encroachments which it makes on the co-ordinate departments."[2] It should be emphasized, however, that Madison did not mean for any branch to act outside its constitutionally prescribed limits. He wrote, "It is agreed on all sides, that the powers properly belonging to one of the departments ought not to be directly and completely administered by either of the other departments."[3] And that included Congress. "I do not conceive that power is given to the President and Senate to dismember the empire, or to alienate any great, essential right. I do not think the whole legislative authority have this power. The exercise of the power must be consistent with the object of the delegation."[4]

John Locke, who was the most widely read philosopher during the American Revolutionary period, explained in his extremely influential *Second Treatise of Government* that a legislative body elected by the people must not delegate the power of lawmaking to any other entity, for that power was delegated to the legislature by the people. Locke wrote, "The legislative cannot transfer the power of making laws to any other hands: for it being but a delegated power from the people, they who have it cannot pass it over to others."[5] He added:

> The power of the legislative, being derived from the people by a positive voluntary grant and institutions, can be no other than what that positive grant conveyed, which being only to make laws, and not to make legislators, the legislative can have no power to transfer their authority of making laws and place it in other hands.[6]

Locke explained that the legislature "is not only the supreme power of the commonwealth, but sacred and unalterable in the hands where the community have one placed it."[7] It is imperative, therefore, that the body chosen by the people, and vested with legislative authority, enact the laws under which the people live. "These are the bounds which the trust, that is put in them by the society, and the law of God and nature, have set to the legislative power of every common-wealth, in all forms of government."[8]

Charles de Montesquieu, who was among the most widely read philosophers during the post-revolutionary period, was hugely influential on the Framers. He is mentioned several times at the Constitutional Convention, in the *Federalist Papers*, and during the state ratification conventions. In his masterpiece, *The Spirit of the Laws*, Montesquieu first expounded on the concept of three distinct governmental branches, each with separate powers to legislate, execute, and adjudicate. He wrote, "When legislative power is united with executive power in a single person or in a simple body of magistracy, there is no liberty, because one can fear that the same monarch or senate that makes tyrannical laws will execute them tyrannically. . . ."[9]

The history and philosophy undergirding the separation-of-powers doctrine, and the unique character of the legislative branch and lawmaking, are unambiguous. As Madison explained in *Federalist* 51: "But what is government itself, but the greatest of all reflections on human nature? If men were angels, no government would be necessary. If angels were to govern men, neither external nor internal controls on government would be necessary. In framing a government which is to be administered by men over men, the great difficulty lies in this: you must first enable the government to control the governed; and in the next place oblige it to control itself."[10] The Framers believed that the institutions of government they had created in the Constitution, and the specific, limited powers they had granted each of them, achieved these ends.

In fact, in 1892, the Supreme Court underscored this most basic understanding when it declared in *Field v. Clark* that the issue of Congress delegating lawmaking authority to the executive branch would raze the constitutional structure the Framers had established. The Court ruled, "That Congress cannot delegate legislative power to the President is a principle universally recognized as vital to the integrity and maintenance of the system of government ordained by the Constitution."[11]

But once again, in the late eighteenth century, as part of the Progressive movement's agenda, a concerted campaign was launched to undo the constitutional construct by concentrating and consolidating power in the federal government. As Woodrow Wilson exclaimed in 1908:

The makers of the federal Constitution followed the scheme as they found it expounded by Montesquieu, followed it with genuine scientific enthusiasm. The admirable expositions of the *Federalist* [*Papers*] read like thoughtful applications of Montesquieu to the political needs and circumstances of America. They are full of the theory of checks and balances. The President is balanced off against Congress, Congress against the President, and each against the courts. . . . Politics is turned into mechanics under this touch. . . . The trouble with the theory is that government is not a machine, but a living thing. . . . It is modified by its environment, necessitated by its tasks, shaped to its functions by sheer pressure of life. No living thing can have its organs offset against each other as checks, and live. . . .[12]

In the 1930s and 1940s, President Franklin Roosevelt launched the New Deal, in which Congress passed laws creating federal agencies and delegating power to them to regulate vast segments of the economy and daily life, in many instances bypassing or supplanting state lawmaking authority. Initially, the Supreme Court struck down a number of these programs—ruling that they went far beyond the authority granted the federal government under the Interstate Commerce Clause—including the Railroad Retirement Act's compulsory retirement plans in *Railroad Retirement Board v. Alton R. Co.*;[13] sections of the National Industrial Recovery Act's wage and hour requirements in *Schechter Poultry Corp. v. United States*;[14] and the Bituminous Coal Conservation Act's establishment of a national coal commission and coal districts as well as the fixing of prices, wages, and hours in *Carter v. Carter Coal Company*.[15]

However, the Court would soon reverse course and abandon its own precedent after Roosevelt threatened to change the Court's makeup. Over time, he did in fact replace the sitting justices with men who shared his ideological views. Subsequently, in the 1937 *Jones v. Laughlin Steel Corp* case, the Court held that "intrastate activities that 'have a close and substantial relation to interstate commerce that their control is essential or appropriate to protect that commerce from burdens and obstructions' are within Congress' power to regulate";[16] later, in the 1942 *Wickard v. Filburn* decision, it went much further, ruling that withholding goods from interstate commerce affects interstate commerce and therefore such activity is subject to congressional lawmaking power.[17]

One of Roosevelt's most prominent advisors, Harvard law professor James Landis, insisted in 1938 that "[i]n terms of political theory, the administrative process springs from the inadequacy of a simple tripartite form of government to deal with modern problems."[18]

These days, each of the federal branches has seized expanded authority over the states and the individual. In addition to Congress's legislative authority, it is now commonplace for the courts to legislate by judicial review and the executive branch to legislate by regulation and executive order. More to the justification of the proposed amendment, the vastness of the federal bureaucracy—that is, an administrative state or what has become a fourth branch of government—destroys the very idea of a representative legislature and does severe damage to the separation-of-powers doctrine. Departments and agencies created by Congress are attached to the executive branch and exercise lawmaking power that is both delegated and not delegated by Congress. And their myriad regulations and rules have the force of law, including criminal and civil penalties. Under present conditions, the administrative state's omnipresence makes congressional oversight, political accountability, and rational reform mostly impracticable if not impossible. And Congress seems more than willing to abandon its core function to the executive branch and accept the status quo, having taken rare and minor steps to rein in the bureaucracy.

Ironically, judicial review, which is exercised vigorously and expansively by the Courts, is all but nonexistent in matters involving congressional delegations to administrative agencies. They mostly defer to the discretion of Congress and, with few exceptions, uphold administrative actions to the extent they consider them seriously at all. Moreover, on those occasions when the Supreme Court does exercise judicial review in these matters, it has been known to extend the power of the administrative state beyond Congress's already broad delegations. For example, in the 2007 case *Massachusetts v. Environmental Protection Agency*, by a 5 to 4 vote the Court actually expanded the Environmental Protection Agency's (EPA) authority to regulate carbon dioxide and other greenhouse gases, despite the agency's long-held determination that these gases are not pollutants subject to regulation. The Court opened the door to an infinite number of agency regulations affecting an endless line of industries, products, and processes.[19]

The modern administrative state has power, resources, and tentacles that boggle the mind. For example, in 2008, the Small Business Administration estimated that annual regulatory compliance costs amounted to $1.752 trillion.[20] In 2012, the Obama administration issued new regulations costing $236 billion. New

EPA regulations alone resulted in $172 billion in regulatory costs.[21]

The 2012 *Federal Register*, the official federal publication documenting administrative rules and proposed rules, exceeded 77,000 pages. The 2011 and 2010 *Federal Registers* were 81,247 and 81,405 pages long, respectively. In 2011, regulatory agencies issued 3,807 final rules, yet Congress passed and the president signed 81 laws.[22] In 2012, the bureaucracy reportedly issued 212 "economically significant" federal rules, each projected to impose more than $100 million in economic costs. In the last ten years, the issuance of economically significant rules has increased 108 percent.[23]

Furthermore, the number of criminal offenses spawned by these regulations, for which citizens are liable, is unknown even to the federal government. The Heritage Foundation observed that "[s]cores of federal departments and agencies have created so many criminal offenses that the Congressional Research Office (CRS) [an arm of Congress] . . . admitted that it was unable to even count all the offenses. The Service's best estimate? 'Tens of thousands.' . . . Congress's own experts do not have a clear understanding of the size and scope of federal criminalization."[24]

Most jarringly, presidents will not hesitate to use the administrative state's rulemaking processes to circumvent Congress when Congress refuses to enact legislation demanded by a president, or does not act quickly enough to satisfy a president's ambitions. Indeed, President Barack Obama has declared repeatedly, including in his 2013 State of the Union speech, that "*if Congress* won't *act* soon to protect future generations, I *will*"—threatening to legislate by executive branch regulation in lieu of congressional action.[25]

The system of federalism is also undermined severely when federal departments and agencies commandeer and preempt state authority, destroying state sovereignty and forcing states into their service—or, conversely, when states surrender their sovereignty in exchange for federal grants and subsidies conditioned on a state's compliance with the mandates of a federal department or agency.

To shed some light on the process, it is worth a brief primer on administrative law—in plain English, of course. Consider that in 1972, Congress passed the Clean Water Act, a law that empowered the EPA to take steps to reduce water pollution by enacting rules or regulations. Once Congress grants such regulatory authority, the agency has discretion to achieve the stated goal.

The actual process of enacting a regulation is somewhat technical. Regulations often originate with what is called an "Advance Notice of Proposed Rulemaking." This initial step consists of a proposal of the action the agency is planning. After a given period of time, the agency releases a "Proposed Rule" for the public to consider and, if moved, submit formal comments. Comments pertaining to a given rule are usually filed by those parties or individuals who have a specific interest in the substance of the rule. The EPA will elicit comments from, say, environmental groups or businesses affected by the regulation. Comments are intended to notify the agency of any legal or perceived legal deficiencies in the proposed rule. Interested parties can notify the agency of widespread support or opposition. The standard time frame for submission of comments to a proposed rule is usually sixty days.[26]

Unfortunately, the process is not always as transparent and professionally objective as might appear on the surface. It can be beset with political and ideological agendas, cronyism, and secret communications, making the comment period a formality, not a serious pursuit of useful information and advice.

The agency has wide latitude in determining when to promulgate a final rule. The Congressional Review Act (CRA) provides that Congress may review these regulations and, if a joint resolution susceptible to a presidential veto passes, the regulation can be overruled.[27] Since 1996, Congress has disapproved only a single rule. Clearly, the CRA is not an effective tool for ensuring congressional oversight or curbing regulatory overreach.

Private parties wishing to challenge the legality of a final rule are obligated generally to file a petition in the U.S. Court of Appeals for the District Columbia Circuit within sixty days of the promulgation of the final rule.[28] Challenging the legality of a regulation is a difficult and expensive process and succeeds in very limited instances. A number of factors make challenging federal regulations in court particularly difficult.

First, the court hearing the challenge presumes, as discussed earlier, that the rule is valid. The private party challenging the regulation must demonstrate that the agency exceeded its rule-making authority. The burden is on private parties to show that the regulation is illegal. Under current law, the reviewing court will rule a given regulation improper if it determines the agency acted in an "arbitrary or capricious" manner or if the agency abused its discretion or acted "not in accordance with the law."[29] Therefore, an agency's regulation will be upheld provided it is rationally based. What constitutes "rationally based" is not always clear, and individuals and groups spend many thousands of dollars on expensive lawyers who attempt to convince courts the agency has acted in an unreasonable manner. It is difficult, if not impossible, for most individuals to husband the resources and expertise to challenge effectively these regulations. Even lawyers who specialize in administrative law often fail. Moreover, most citizens have no idea that rules that may affect their daily lives are being promulgated, given the insular nature of the process, the quantity of regulations being issued, and the news media's disinterest.

Second, courts have dismissed categorically the allegation that a particular agency action constitutes impermissible legislative activity. In other words, courts reject the argument that Congress cannot delegate its core function of legislating to an executive branch entity—known as the *nondelegation doctrine*. The Constitution's plain language makes clear that Congress is vested with "all legislative powers herein granted." But the Supreme Court has declared the doctrine unworkable, which, in turn, damages the separation-of-powers doctrine. The Court, which often exercises judicial review in an activist fashion, believes it is "almost never qualified to second-guess Congress regarding the permissible degree of policy judgment that can be left to those executing or applying the law."[30]

Another factor favoring federal agency rulemaking authority is the overwhelming deference paid by the courts to the agency's positions. When private entities challenge a given regulation, they often allege that the agency acted improperly. Under a Supreme Court–invented legal standard known as the *Chevron* doctrine, when Congress passes a broadly worded law, the agency's interpretation of what the law means will be controlling unless such interpretation is unreasonable.[31] Thus, for example, Congress passes a generic, benign statute and delegates the authority to work out the details of the law to the federal bureaucracy, which is not accountable to the electorate. Lower courts, which often hear cases involving regulatory challenges, are bound by the *Chevron* doctrine and will uphold agency regulations in all but the most extraordinary challenges.

There are numerous regulations that exceed their respective statutory mandates—so many, in fact, that they cannot all be discussed here. However, a group of recent environmental regulations—recently upheld as valid by the D.C. Circuit Court of Appeals—illustrate the desirability of the proposed amendment.

In 1970, Congress passed significant amendments to the Clean Air Act (CAA) that were designed to reduce air pollution from stationary sources, such as factories and power plants, and mobile sources, such as cars and airplanes.[32] The newly created EPA was tasked with enforcing and administering the law. Congress passed additional amendments to the CAA in 1973 and 1990. Each time, Congress decided to expand the EPA's authority to regulate a growing number of hazardous substances.

Fast-forward to 2009: carbon emissions, a very small fraction of greenhouse gas emissions (GHGs), became the target of, among others, the environmental movement. But Congress refused to pass new legislation expanding the CAA's coverage to include greenhouse gases, for they are not pollutants. Nevertheless, then–EPA administrator Lisa Jackson, admitting the CAA was not an "ideal tool," decided she would use the more than forty-year-old statute for curbing carbon emissions. As such, she and the president were bypassing Congress. Congress chose to do nothing about it.

The CAA's provisions are not designed for carbon regulation. For example, a program operated under the CAA known as the Prevention of Significant Deterioration (PSD) mandates specific pollution thresholds for triggering regulatory requirements.[33] These thresholds are detailed in the statute itself. Therefore, if a power plant emits 250 tons per year of a pollutant, the PSD program obligates that power plant to take costly steps to remediate the pollution.[34] Congress considered the merits of setting the threshold numbers and passed a statute setting those numbers. Hence, Congress does have the practical capacity to do such things. When the EPA decided to use the CAA as legal justification for instituting regulations relating to greenhouse gas emissions, the EPA was obligated to comply with that law's provisions. Greenhouse gases are emitted by stationary sources, even HVAC systems, numbering in the millions.[35] All of these sources emit GHGs in excess of 250 tons per year. Since the PSD program was expanded at the instigation of the EPA and not by statute, the EPA would logically have to regulate these millions of stationary sources.

But realizing the impossibility of the task, Jackson noted that the CAA was not the proper law for regulating GHGs. Consequently, she decided the EPA would discard existing statutory law and set new regulatory thresholds for GHGs. When challenged, the D.C. Circuit upheld the changes, deferring to the EPA's authority.

Another example: On March 22, 2010, Congress passed Obamacare, a bill some 2,700 pages long.[36] An analysis by Peter Ferrara of the Heartland Institute concludes the law establishes more than "150 new bureaucracies, agencies, boards, commissions and programs" that "are empowered to tell doctors and hospitals what is quality health care and what is not, what are best practices in medicine, how their medical practices should be structured, and what they will be paid and when."[37] The Congressional Research Service reported, "The precise number of new entities that will ultimately be created . . . is currently unknowable."[38] The regulatory burden and cost will be enormous.[39] And during the early stages of the law's implementation, the executive branch has already issued twenty thousand pages of regulations and thousands more to come.[40] Initial Internal Revenue Service regulations alone amount to 159 pages.[41]

When Congress passed Obamacare it attempted by statute to confer fundamental legislative powers on the executive branch, and even sought to prohibit future Congresses from altering its unconstitutional act. Specifically, Congress created the fifteen-member Independent Payment Advisory Board (IPAB), which ostensibly is responsible for controlling Medicare costs. The board submits a proposal to Congress, which automatically becomes law, and the Department of Health and Human Services must implement it, unless the proposal is affirmatively blocked by Congress and the president. Even then, it can be stopped only if the elected branches agree on a substitute. Obamacare also attempts to prohibit citizens from challenging the board's decisions in court. Moreover, Obamacare seeks to tie the hands of future Congresses by forbidding Congress from dissolving the board outside of a seven-month period in 2017, and only by a supermajority three-fifths vote of both houses. If Congress does not act in that time frame, Congress is prohibited from even altering a board proposal.[42]

Apart from all the rest, the abuse of power by one Congress and president in attempting to reorganize the federal government and redraft fundamentally the Constitution outside of the amendment processes, with the intention of binding all future Congresses in perpetuity and leaving citizens with no political or legal recourse, is simply sinister. But it underscores the Statists' contempt for the Constitution and self-government.

Shortly thereafter, on July 21, 2010, the same Congress passed, and the president signed, the Dodd-Frank Wall Street Reform and Consumer Protection Act, aka Dodd-Frank, supposedly intended to protect the consumer from risky decisions by financial institutions.[43] The law is as offensive to the Constitution as Obamacare, again violating separation of powers and insulating broad policy-making decisions from the citizenry.

For example, under Dodd-Frank, Congress established the Consumer Financial Protection Bureau (CFPB), which has open-ended power to prevent certain financial institutions from committing or engaging in "unfair," "deceptive," or "abusive" practices respecting a consumer financial product or service. No statutory definition for "unfair" or "deceptive" acts or practices is provided. The CFPB has exclusive authority to prescribe rules, issue guidance, conduct examinations, require reports, or issue exemptions, with little legal recourse by those affected by its decisions.[44]

Moreover, Congress has no appropriating authority over the CFPB, for the law authorizes the CFPB to fund itself by unilaterally claiming funds from the Federal Reserve Board. The director of the CFPB alone determines the amount of funding the CFPB receives from the Fed. The law also prohibits explicitly the House and Senate appropriations committees from even attempting to "review" the CFPB's budget. And the director receives a five-year term. He can be removed by the president only "for inefficiency, neglect of duty, or malfeasance in office."[45]

In addition, Congress established the fifteen-member Financial Stability Oversight Council and granted it broad executive powers. It has open-ended discretion to designate nonbank financial institutions "systemically important," from which flows wide-ranging regulatory authority over these businesses. The law

actually prohibits aggrieved parties from challenging the legal suf-
ficiency of the council's actions and conclusions in court.[46]

The delegation of colossal power to an administrative state,
authority the Constitution grants to individual branches of the
federal government, violates the separation-of-powers doctrine,
including Congress's legislative authority and power over the public purse, and presidential prerogatives in determining whether
to fire an executive branch employee; it also thwarts the public's
ability to participate in major legal, social, cultural, and economic
decisions affecting their lives through the grant and expansion of
lawmaking power in bureaucratic fiefdoms largely immune from
legislative oversight and input. Plain and simple, this is further
evidence of the dissolution of constitutional republicanism.

It would seem counterintuitive for Congress to surrender its
own power to executive branch entities of its own making, and
for a president to surrender his own decision-making authority
to an administrative state. But if the purpose is to centralize and
concentrate power in the federal government, in defiance of our
founding principles and the Constitution—as the Statists have
preached and promoted actively for more than a century—then
the frequent and broad delegation of lawmaking power to a permanent, ever-present federal bureaucracy, insulated from public
influence, makes perfect sense.

The proposed amendment eschews the issue of delegation
per se, the total reversal of which would seem impossible at this
point, but importantly, it returns final decision-making authority
respecting laws (regulations and rules) with significant economic
impact to Congress, thereby restoring a critical element of separa-

tion of powers under the Constitution and reinvigorating representative government. The proposed amendment sunsets every executive federal department and agency and obligates Congress to determine the efficacy of each entity every three years. It also establishes a permanent joint committee, which makes final determinations respecting the most economically costly federal regulations. The proposed amendment does not prevent Congress from otherwise abolishing or creating federal departments or agencies, modifying their missions, or affecting their directions, policies, and funding. However, given Congress's abandonment of its core constitutional duty, thereby gutting the fundamental nature of representative government, the proposed amendment is among the only ways to rebalance the legislative function of the federal government.

The proposed amendment embraces the Framers' original plan: Congress legislates, not administrative agencies within the executive branch. It obligates Congress to undertake the duties intended by the Framers and set forth in the Constitution, prohibiting it from delegating and abdicating final authority over major laws.

CHAPTER SEVEN

An Amendment to Promote Free Enterprise

SECTION 1: Congress's power to regulate Commerce is not a plenary grant of power to the federal government to regulate and control economic activity but a specific grant of power limited to preventing states from impeding commerce and trade between and among the several States.

SECTION 2: Congress's power to regulate Commerce does not extend to activity within a state, whether or not it affects interstate commerce; nor does it extend to compelling an individual or entity to participate in commerce or trade.

THE CONSTITUTION'S COMMERCE CLAUSE states that Congress shall have the power "[t]o regulate Commerce with foreign Nations, and among the several States, and with the Indian Tribes."[1] The proposed amendment focuses on that part of the clause respecting Congress's power to regulate commerce among the several states and addresses the federal government's ever-expanding involvement in and interference with private economic activity and property rights. It is at first essential to understand what the Framers meant by these words and the Framers' purpose.

In 1996, the late constitutional scholar and Harvard law professor Raoul Berger explained that

> [t]he focus on trade alone was not fortuitous; the Framers were fastidious in their choice of words. For them, "trade" did not, for example, include agricultural production, which plainly was "local." In the Convention, George Mason said that the "general government could not know how to make laws for every part [state]—such as respects agriculture." And [Alexander] Hamilton wrote in *Federalist* No. 17 that "the supervision of agriculture and of other concerns of a similar nature . . . which are proper to be provided for by local legislation, *can never be desirable* cares of a general jurisdiction." In *Federalist* No. 12, he adverted to the "rivalship that once subsisted" between agriculture and commerce. . . . Hamilton referred separately in *Federalist* No. 36 to "agriculture, commerce, [and] manufactures" as "different . . . kinds" of "wealth, property, and industry," not as fused in commerce. In sum, the Founders conceived of "commerce" as "trade," the interchange of goods by one State with another.[2]

Berger added:

The Founders' all-but-exclusive concern was with exactions
by some states from their neighbors. [James] Madison said,
"It would be unjust to the States whose produce was ex-
ported by their neighbours, to leave it subject to be taxed by
the latter." [James] Wilson "dwelt on the injustice and im-
policy of leaving New Jersey[,] Connecticut &c any longer
subject to the exactions of their commercial neighbours."
That the Commerce Clause was meant to remedy this mischief is clear. Madison stated that it was necessary to remove "existing & injurious retaliations *among* the States,"
that "the best guard against [this 'abuse'] was the right in
the Genl. Government to regulate trade *between* State and
State." [Roger] Sherman stated that "the oppression of the
uncommercial States was guarded agst. by the power to regulate *trade between* the States." And Oliver Elseworth said
that the "power of regulating trade between the States will
protect them agst each other." Given the jealous attachment
to state sovereignty, the absence of objection that the Commerce Clause invaded State autonomy indicates that such
an intrusion was simply unimaginable. [Thomas] Jefferson
accurately reflected the Founders' views when he stated in
1791 that "the power given to Congress by the Constitution
does not extend to the internal regulation of the commerce
of a state . . . which remains exclusively with its own legislature; but to its external commerce only, that is to say, its
commerce with another state, or with foreign nations. . . ."
That no more was intended was made clear by Madison in

a letter to J. C. Cabell: "*among* the several States" . . . grew out of the abuses of the power by the importing States in taxing the non-importing, and was intended as a negative and preventive provision against injustice among the States themselves, rather than as a power to be used for the positive purposes of the General Government. . . .[3]

In 2001, Commerce Clause expert and Georgetown University law professor Randy E. Barnett undertook an extensive examination of the original meaning of the Constitution's Commerce Clause and the Framers' intent. Having also returned to the Constitutional Convention and the *Federalist Papers*, as well as the state ratification debates, Barnett "found . . . that the term 'commerce' was consistently used in the narrow sense and that *there is no surviving example of it being used in either source in any broader sense*. The same holds true for the use of the word 'commerce' in the *Federalist Papers*."[4]

Barnett wrote, "In Madison's notes for the Constitutional Convention, the term 'commerce' appears thirty-four times in the speeches of the delegates. Eight of these are unambiguous references to commerce with foreign nations which can only consist of trade. In every other instance, the terms 'trade' or 'exchange' could be substituted for the term 'commerce' with the apparent meaning of the statement preserved. In no instance is the term 'commerce' clearly used to refer to 'any gainful activity' or anything broader than trade."[5] Barnett continued, "In none of the sixty-three appearances of the term 'commerce' in the *Federalist Papers* is it ever used to unambiguously refer to any activity beyond trade or exchange."[6] Furthermore, he wrote, "Having examined every use of the term 'commerce' that appears in the reports of the state ratification conventions, I found that the term was uniformly used to refer to trade or exchange, rather than all gainful activity."[7] In the end, writes Barnett, "if anyone in the Constitutional Convention or the state ratification conventions used the term 'commerce' to refer to something more comprehensive than 'trade' or 'exchange,' they either failed to make explicit that meaning or their comments were not recorded for posterity."[8]

In 2002, the late constitutional scholar Robert H. Bork and attorney Daniel E. Troy, also examining the Constitution's Commerce Clause, explained:

> Early American writings distinguish "commerce" from the class of subjects to which it is separate but connected in two ways: either by a direct discussion of what is excluded from commerce, or by implication. Alexander Hamilton's writings in *The Federalist Papers* provide many of these definitions by implication. Hamilton often included "commerce" in a list of concepts which are similar in one way (activities critical to the success of the nation, for instance), but distinct enough to call for separate identification, as in "the state of commerce, of arts, of industry." These early discussions of the nature of the Union suggest that "commerce" does not include manufacturing, agriculture, labor, or industry. In short, "commerce" does not seem to have been used during the founding era to refer to those acts that precede the act of trade. Interstate commerce seems to refer to interstate trade—that is, commerce is "intercourse for the purposes of trade in any and all its forms, including the transportation, purchase, sale, and exchange of commodities between the . . . citizens of different States."[9]

In fact, time and again the Framers made clear their intentions. In *Federalist* 42, Madison stated, in part: "A very material object of this power was the relief of the States which import and export through other States from the improper contributions levied on them by the latter. Were these at liberty to regulate the trade between State and State, it must be foreseen that ways would be found out to load the articles of import and export, during the passage through their jurisdiction, with duties which would fall on the makers of the latter and the consumers of the former."[10] In *Federalist* 45, Madison wrote famously that "[t]he powers delegated by the proposed Constitution to the federal government are few and defined. Those which are to remain in the State governments are numerous and indefinite."[11]

For the Framers, promoting and securing commerce and trade were not matters of theoretical and academic debate but national survival. They were addressing a dire problem that threatened the existence of the country following the Revolutionary War. The young nation was weak economically. The country barely survived war with one of the world's superpowers, Great Britain. The individual states had often functioned like individual countries and were given to frequent squabbles. Now the fledgling nation found itself surrounded by European powers in Canada, Florida, and Louisiana. In an age of mercantilism, Europe sought advantages in trade by excluding American businesses and promoting their own.[12] The states themselves, although joined together in 1781 by the Articles of Confederation, sought to gain advantage over each other with tariffs and regulations.[13] States even printed their own currency, which added to the confusion.[14]

It is difficult to see how America could have long survived under this type of system. Yet this was the state of American enterprise in the early days of the republic. As Associate Justice Joseph Story observed:

> It is hardly possible to exaggerate the oppressed and degraded
> state of domestic commerce, manufactures, and agriculture, at
> the time of the adoption of the Constitution. Our ships were
> almost driven from the ocean; our work-shops were nearly
> deserted; our mechanics were in a starving condition; and
> our agriculture was sunk to the lowest ebb. These were the
> natural results of the inability of the General Government to
> regulate commerce, so as to prevent the injurious monopolies
> and exclusions of foreign nations, and the conflicting, and
> often ruinous regulations of the different States.[15]

Story's commentaries on the Constitution are considered some of the most significant early works on the subject. It is important to note that Story, although writing in the 1800s, used the language typical of the time of the Constitution's drafting and ratification.[16] Commerce, manufacturing, and agriculture were separate and distinct areas of economic activity, as is plain from, among other things, their multiple references in the *Federalist Papers*.[17] "Commerce" was not a catchall to describe all three. If commerce was not agriculture or manufacturing, then it would indicate that the Framers did not intend the federal government to regulate without severe and effective limits. The separation of the three concepts, in other words, indicates a significant and purposeful limitation to the commerce power.

Indeed, commerce was so important in the early days that it was a catalyst for the Constitutional Convention. In 1786, Virginia invited the other states to a meeting in Annapolis, Maryland, to deal with commercial issues. That September, several delegates met but realized that commerce could not be separated from larger issues of governance. They called for another convention and returned to their states.[18] Congress agreed and, of course, in 1787 representatives convened in Philadelphia at what would later be known as the Constitutional Convention.

James Madison, among others, had been troubled by the many deficiencies in the Articles of Confederation, including their detrimental effect on commerce. In 1787, he wrote a critique of the Articles, listing their many "vices." Within a section focusing on "Trespasses of the States on the rights of each other," he identified how the individual states had been engaging in trade wars.

> The practice of many States in restricting the commercial intercourse with other States, and putting their productions and manufactures on the same footing with those of foreign nations, though not contrary to the federal articles, is certainly adverse to the spirit of the Union, and tends to beget retaliating regulations, not less expensive & vexatious in themselves, than they are destructive of the general harmony.[19]

States with navigable ports extracted taxes from adjoining states, whose merchants were exporting their goods to foreign markets. States taxed imported goods from other states and, in some instances, at rates even higher than foreign countries. In the preface to the debates, Madison laid the problem bare:

> [T]he States having ports for foreign commerce, taxed & irritated the adjoining States, trading thro' them, as N.Y. Pena. Virga. & S—Carolina. Some of the States, as Con-

necticut, taxed imports as from Massts higher than imports
even from G.B. of wch Massts. complained to Virga. and
doubtless to other States. In sundry instances of as N.Y. N.J.
Pa. & Maryd. the navigation laws treated the Citizens of
other States as aliens.[20]

The *Federalist Papers*, designed to rally support behind state
ratification, mentioned frequently the importance of a national
commercial system without internal barriers. In *Federalist* 11,
"The Utility of the Union in Respect to Commercial Relations
and a Navy," Alexander Hamilton wrote:

> An unrestrained intercourse between the States themselves
> will advance the trade of each by an interchange of their
> respective productions, not only for the supply of reciprocal
> wants at home, but for exportation to foreign markets. The
> veins of commerce in every part will be replenished, and
> will acquire additional motion and vigor from a free circula-
> tion of the commodities of every part.[21]

A common thread in the critiques of the Articles of Confederation and the arguments in support of the Constitution is that
the Framers wanted to *promote* commerce. The Commerce Clause
was the solution to a specific problem: the erection of trade barriers that threatened commerce and trade. The Framers did not say
that the Articles of Confederation were deficient because Congress
lacked the power to set wages for workers or limit how much wheat
a farmer could grow. If anyone suggested such a thing in Philadelphia, he might have been tarred and feathered. At the very least,
the Commerce Clause would never have survived state ratifica-

tion. Put another way, the Framers did not empower the federal government, in small ways and large, to control the economy for whatever good and promised ends federal officials might proclaim.

This understanding of the limited powers of the Commerce Clause was actually reflected in the decisions of the Supreme Court for most of our history—up to 1937. Although the Court struggled with various factual scenarios in applying the clause, and constructed different tests for that purpose, to its credit the Court mostly attempted to honor the text of the clause and the Framers' intent.

In 1824, the Court first addressed the Commerce Clause in *Gibbons v. Ogden*. In that case, New York had granted exclusive navigation rights to its waterways to Robert R. Livingston and Robert Fulton for boats powered by "fire or steam." Congress, however, had passed a law in 1793 regulating coastal trade. The Court, under Chief Justice John Marshall, considered whether the power to regulate commerce included the power to regulate navigation. While holding that it did, Marshall noted that Congress could regulate "navigation" because "[a]ll America . . . has uniformly understood, the word 'commerce,' to comprehend navigation. It was so understood, and must have been so understood, when the constitution was framed."[22] But the Court also noted that this power to regulate commerce "among the several states" did not extend to purely internal commerce.

> Comprehensive as the word "among" is, it may very properly be restricted to that commerce which concerns more States than one. . . . The genius and character of the whole government seem to be, that its action is to be applied to all the external concerns of the nation, and to those internal concerns which affect the States generally; but not to those which

are completely within a particular State, which do not affect other States, and with which it is not necessary to interfere, for the purpose of executing some of the general powers of the government. *The completely internal commerce of a State, then, may be considered as reserved for the State itself.*[23]

New York's attempt to grant a monopoly over navigation rights was struck down. The limitations on the Commerce Clause acknowledged by *Gibbons v. Ogden* were generally followed by the Court for well over one hundred years.

Even during the earliest days of the New Deal, the Supreme Court acknowledged the limits the Commerce Clause placed on Congress and the president. Congress had passed a number of laws and established several new agencies that centralized within the federal government decision-making on a broad spectrum of economic matters having nothing to do with commerce among the several states. In 1934, Congress passed the Railroad Retirement Act, which established compulsory retirement plans for railroad workers. The Court invalidated it in 1935 because Congress had no constitutional authority to regulate a business relationship between employer and employee. The Court wrote, "We feel bound to hold that a pension plan thus imposed is in no proper sense a regulation of the activity of interstate transportation. It is an attempt for social ends to impose by sheer fiat non-contractual incidents upon the relation of employer and employee, not as a rule of regulation or commerce or transportation between the States, but as a means of assuring a particular class of employees against old age dependency."[24]

Thereafter, the Court struck down sections of the National Industrial Recovery Act of 1933 in the *Schechter Poultry* or "sick chicken" case, holding that the Commerce Clause did not em-

power Congress to enact a law setting wages and hours of poultry
workers in Brooklyn, New York. The Court also found that the
chickens never left the state, writing, in part: "So far as the poultry here in question is concerned, the flow in interstate commerce
had ceased. The poultry had come to permanent rest within the
state. It was held, used or sold by defendants in relation to any
further transaction in interstate commerce and was not destined
for transportation to other states." The Court declared, "If the
commerce clause were construed to reach all enterprises and
transactions which could be said to have an indirect effect upon
interstate commerce, the federal authority would embrace practically all the activities of the people."[25]

In 1936, the Court ruled that another New Deal law, the Bituminous Coal Conservation Act, was unconstitutional. The act
created a national coal commission, as well as coal districts, and
fixed coal prices, wages, hours, and working conditions of miners
throughout the country. The Court concluded:

> Much stress is put upon the evils which come from the
> struggle between employers and employees over the mat-
> ter of wages, working conditions, the right of collective
> bargaining, etc., and the resulting strikes, curtailment and
> irregularity of production and effects on prices; and it is in-
> sisted that interstate commerce is greatly affected thereby.
> But, in addition to what has just been said, the conclusive
> answer is that the evils are all local evils over which the
> federal government has no legislative control.[26]

President Franklin Roosevelt struck back. He threatened to
pack the Supreme Court and did, in fact, begin to change its

makeup by replacing retiring justices with lawyers who shared his contempt for the constitution's enumeration of limited federal powers. It was not long before the Court abruptly reversed course.

It began with the 1937 decision in *Jones v. Laughlin Steel Corp.*, where the Court ruled that intrastate activities that "have a close and substantial relation to interstate commerce [such] that their control is essential or appropriate to protect that commerce from burdens and obstructions" are within Congress's power to regulate.[27]

The legal stage was now set for a radical departure from the Constitution's Commerce Clause text and the Framers' intent.

The most infamous of the Court's New Deal decisions in this regard came in 1942 with its ruling in *Wickard v. Filburn*. In this case, the Court abandoned any semblance of jurisprudential integrity and joined with the rest of the federal government in unleashing what is today an endless array of federal interventions in private economic activity.[28]

The *Wickard* case involved a dairy farm in Ohio owned by Roscoe Filburn. He used a portion of his land to grow wheat. Every year the wheat he produced was used in four ways: some was sold, some was fed to his livestock, some was used to make flour, and the rest was used for seeding for the following year. The use or sale of his wheat all occurred exclusively within the state of Ohio. The Agricultural Adjustment Act of 1938, however, set quotas on the amount of wheat he was allowed to produce. When Filburn exceeded the quota, he was fined by the federal government.

How could the federal government regulate wheat that was grown, used, and sold wholly within the borders of Ohio? The Supreme Court wrote, in part:

It can hardly be denied that a factor of such volume and
variability as home-consumed wheat would have a substantial influence on price and market conditions. This may
arise because being in marketable condition such wheat
overhangs the market and if induced by rising prices tends
to flow into the market and check price increases. But if we
assume that it is never marketed, it supplied a need of the
man who grew it which would otherwise be reflected by purchases in the open market. Home-grown wheat in this sense
competes with wheat in commerce. The stimulation of commerce is a use of the regulatory function quite as definitely as
prohibitions or restrictions on them.[29]

If there was any doubt at all where the Court was taking the
nation, it added that "even if appellee's activity be local and
though it may not be regarded as commerce, it may still, whatever its nature, be reached by Congress if it exerts a substantial
economic effect on interstate commerce. . . ."[30] Hence, noncom-
mercial, local activity could be regulated by the federal government if it was said to have a substantial effect on commerce, even
when it did not. Consequently, virtually any economic activity
could be said to affect interstate commerce.

For the last seventy years, since the *Wickard* decision, Congress
has passed laws and federal departments and agencies have issued
regulations affecting all manner of economic activity. Rather than
promoting private commerce and trade without barriers between and
among the states, which was the indisputable rationale for the Commerce Clause, the federal government now intervenes in private
economic activity, and stomps on state sovereignty, at every turn.

For example, in 1968, in *Maryland v. Wirtz*, the Supreme

Court ruled that the federal Fair Labor Standards Act applied to state-run hospitals, nursing care facilities, and schools because "labor conditions in schools and hospitals can affect commerce."[31] It added that if Congress had a "rational basis" for enacting the law, the Court would uphold it.[32]

In 1971, in *Perez v. United States*, the Court upheld provisions of the Consumer Credit Protection Act, making loan-sharking a federal offense despite the fact that these activities occurred strictly at the local level. The Court ruled, "Extortionate credit transactions, though purely intrastate, may, in the judgment of Congress affect interstate commerce."[33] In his lone dissent, Associate Justice Potter Stewart argued that

> under the statue before us, a man can be convicted without any proof of interstate movement, of the use of the facilities of interstate commerce, or of facts showing that his conduct affected interstate commerce. I think the Framers of the Constitution never intended that the National Government might define as a crime and prosecute wholly local activity through the enactment of federal criminal laws.[34]

With rare exceptions, the Court has generally held that any federal law could affect commerce and would be constitutionally sustained, if Congress provides a "rational basis" for a given law's impact on interstate commerce. Of course, most laws are based on some rational basis. Otherwise, they would be irrational. That is a very low bar indeed.

In fact, there have been only two clear instances since *Wickard* where the Supreme Court has actually rejected Congress's attempt to further expand its power through the Commerce Clause.

In 1995, in *U.S. v. Lopez*, Congress attempted to make the possession of a firearm near a school a federal crime with the Gun-Free
Schools Zone Act of 1990. Proponents of the measure argued,
among other things, that the inherent dangers of guns would increase insurance costs or deter travel, or that guns near schools
would have a detrimental effect on education, a necessary foundation of commercial and economic activity. The Court found these
arguments beyond the reach of the Commerce Clause. As Chief
Justice William Rehnquist wrote, the possession of a firearm near
a school did not meet even the Court's extremely broad view of
commerce, which he summarized as follows:

> First, Congress may regulate the use of the channels of in-
> terstate commerce. . . . Second, Congress is empowered
> to regulate and protect the instrumentalities of interstate
> commerce, or persons or things in interstate commerce,
> even though the threat may come only from intrastate
> activities. . . . Finally, Congress' commerce authority in-
> cludes the power to regulate those activities having a sub-
> stantial relation to interstate commerce, . . . i.e., those
> activities that substantially affect interstate commerce. . . .[35]

Notably, even when drawing a line against Congress's power
grab, Rehnquist embraced the Court's earlier distortion of the
Commerce Clause in *Wickard*.

Moreover, consider Associate Justice Stephen Breyer's outlook
in his dissent.

> Congress obviously could have thought that guns and learn-
> ing are mutually exclusive. Congress could therefore have

found a substantial educational problem—teachers unable to teach, students unable to learn—and concluded that guns near schools contribute substantially to the size and scope of that problem. Having found that guns in schools significantly undermine the quality of education in our Nation's classrooms, Congress could also have found, given the effect of education upon interstate and foreign commerce, that gun-related violence in and around schools is a commercial, as well as human, problem. Education, although far more than a matter of economics, has long been inextricably intertwined with the Nation's economy.[36]

For Breyer, there simply are no real limits on Congress's power to intervene in private economic behavior. Of course, state and local governments have the authority to outlaw gun possession near schools and often do. But Breyer was not alone. Associate Justice David Souter considered the Court's pre-1937 efforts to comply with the Commerce Clause's text and history "the old judicial pretension [that was] discredited and abandoned,"[37] from which "the Court extricated itself almost 60 years ago" by discarding its "untenable jurisprudence."[38] Associate Justice Anthony Kennedy, although concurring with the Court's holding, wrote that "*stare decisis* [the Court's precedent] . . . counsel[s] us not to call into question the essential principles now in place. . . ."[39] It "forecloses us from reverting to an understanding of commerce that would serve only an 18th-century economy."[40]

Consequently, Souter rejected flatly what he knew to be the unequivocal intention of the Framers when fashioning the Commerce Clause, and Kennedy determined that the only judicial precedents worthy of faithful adherence were Commerce Clause opinions the Court began issuing in 1937. As for economic growth necessitating the rewrite of the Commerce Clause, Raoul Berger noted that these justices "too easily assume that economic growth necessarily is accompanied by automatic expansion of the Constitution to facilitate it. Economic expansion, however, cannot alter the scope of the 'fixed' Constitution, particularly when the alteration constitutes a federal takeover of functions that the states were assured were 'inviolable.' "[41] In fact, the industrial revolution in the United States predated the New Deal, turning the nation into the most powerful economic force on earth and creating a vast middle class.

The second case, *United States v. Morrison*, came in 2000 and involved the Violence Against Women Act of 1994, which created a federal cause of action for victims of gender-based violence. If upheld, Congress would have assumed police powers belonging to the states and localities, and the authority to federalize virtually any criminal activity. However, the Court found the link between the statute and interstate commerce too ephemeral. Rehnquist wrote:

> We accordingly reject that argument that Congress may regulate noneconomic, violent criminal conduct based solely on that conduct's aggregate effect on interstate commerce. The Constitution requires a distinction between what is truly national and what is truly local.[42]

In his dissent, Breyer noted correctly that the Court had not rejected its post-1937 precedent but he complained that it had not expanded that precedent far enough.

The Court's rules, even if broadly interpreted, are under-inclusive. The local pickpocket is no less a traditional subject of state regulation than is the local gender-motivated assault. Regardless, the Court reaffirms, as it should, Congress' well-established and frequently exercised power to enact laws that satisfy a commerce-related jurisdictional prerequisite—for example, that some item relevant to the federally regulated activity has at some time crossed a state line. . . . And in a world where most everyday products or their component parts cross interstate boundaries, Congress will frequently find it possible to redraft a statute using language that ties the regulation to the interstate movement of some relevant object, thereby regulating local criminal activity or, for that matter, family affairs.[43]

The ruling did not slow Congress's march for ever more authority to control economic activity and the states. And, as Breyer suggested, Congress would move to regulate family matters. Most recently and notoriously, in its Obamacare decision, four of the nine Supreme Court justices were prepared to use the Commerce Clause to uphold a provision in the law, the so-called individual mandate, penalizing individuals who refuse to engage in an economic transaction against their wishes and/or interests—that is, the purchase of a private health-care policy. As written, Obamacare imposes a "penalty" on those uninsured individuals who do not purchase health insurance. These four justices would have upheld the law on Commerce Clause grounds, insisting that a decision by an individual not to take any action affects interstate commerce. In a four-justice concurring opinion, Associate Justice

Ruth Bader Ginsburg wrote, "[T]he decision to forgo insurance is hardly inconsequential or equivalent to 'doing nothing,' . . . it is, instead, an economic decision Congress has the authority to address under the Commerce Clause."[44] It would seem the nation is one Supreme Court justice away from the federal government dictating all manner of individual behavior.[45]

Lest we forget, the Supreme Court is ruling on laws passed by Congress and regulations issued by the executive branch. Since 1937, all three branches of the federal government have colluded openly in dismantling the Constitution's structure. The governing masterminds, elected and appointed, have bulldozed through the enumeration of powers, separation of powers, and the states' sovereignty to regulate and control private economic activity— and more. The rewriting of the Constitution without benefit of constitutional amendment is behavior that is, by definition, unconstitutional.

The proposed amendment returns the power to regulate commerce and trade to one of defined parameters. It not only encourages commerce and trade between and among the states but, as the Framers understood and intended, also preserves the civil society and promotes individual liberty. This is a hugely significant matter. As Dr. Milton Friedman explained: "Freedom in economic arrangements is itself a component of freedom broadly understood, so economic freedom is an end in itself. . . . [E]conomic freedom is also an indispensable means toward the achievement of political freedom."[46]

CHAPTER EIGHT

AN AMENDMENT TO
PROTECT PRIVATE PROPERTY

SECTION 1: When any governmental entity acts not to secure a private property right against actions that injure property owners, but to take property for a public use from a property owner by actual seizure or through regulation, which taking results in a market value reduction of the property, interference with the use of the property, or a financial loss to the property owner exceeding $10,000, the government shall compensate fully said property owner for such losses.

INFLUENCED BY LUMINARIES SUCH as John Locke and William Blackstone, the Founders understood that the fundamental right to own and maintain property was an essential element in a functioning civil society. In *The Second Treatise of Government,* which was hugely popular during the American founding and heavily relied on by Thomas Jefferson in drafting the Declaration of Independence, Locke asserted:

> [The government] cannot take from any man any part of his property without his own consent. For the preservation of property being the end of government, and that for which men enter into society it necessarily supposes and requires, that the people should have property, without which they must be suppos'd to lose that by entering into society, which was the end for which they entered into it, too gross an absurdity for any man to own.[1]

In his celebrated *Commentaries on the Laws of England*, Blackstone also extols the right to property:

> So great . . . is the regard of the law for private property, that it will not authorize the least violation of it; no, not even for the general good of the whole community. If a new road, for instance, were to be made through the grounds of a private person, it might perhaps be extensively beneficial to the public; but the law permits no man, or set of men, to do this without consent of the owner of the land.[2]

Blackstone added that "the public good is in nothing more essentially interested, than in the protection of every individual's private right, as modeled by the municipal law."[3]

Owning and preserving property free from oppressive government intrusion serves as one of the fundamental building blocks for a prosperous republic. James Madison noted, "Government is instituted no less for protection of property than of the persons, of individuals."[4] In short, property rights are unalienable rights. "The rights of property are committed into the same hands with the personal rights. Some attention ought, therefore, to be paid to property in the choice of those hands."[5] Gouverneur Morris, a widely influential Founder, observed that enshrining property rights in a civil society was a necessary antecedent to any concept of a functioning community. "Without society property in goods is extremely precarious. There is not even the idea of property in lands."[6] Like Madison, Morris believed that an elemental purpose of any legitimate government was the preservation of property. "Conventions to defend each other's goods naturally apply to the defense of those places where the goods are deposited. The object of such conventions must be to preserve for each his own share."[7] Thus, "property is the principal cause and object of society."[8]

George Mason declared in the Virginia Declaration of Rights, the precursor to the Declaration of Independence, that "all men are by nature equally free and independent and have certain inherent rights . . . namely the enjoyment of life and liberty, with the means of acquiring and possessing property. . . ."[9]

Perhaps John Adams put it best when he wrote:

Suppose a nation, rich and poor, high and low, ten millions in number, all assembled together; not more than one or two millions will have lands, houses, or any personal property; if we take into the account the women and children, or even if we leave them out of the question, a great majority of every nation is wholly destitute of property, except a small quantity of clothes, and a few trifles of other movables. Would Mr. Nedham be responsible that, if all were to be decided by a vote of the majority, the eight or nine millions who have no property, would not think of usurping over the rights of the one or two millions who have? Property is surely a right of mankind as really as liberty. Perhaps, at first, prejudice, habit, shame or fear, principle or religion, would restrain the poor from attacking the rich, and the idle from usurping on the industrious; but the time would not be long before courage and enterprise would come, and pretexts be invented by degrees, to countenance the majority in dividing all the property among them, or at least, in sharing it equally with its present possessors. Debts would be abolished first; taxes laid heavy on the rich, and not at all on the others; and at last a downright equal division of every thing be demanded, and voted. What would be the consequence of this? The idle, the vicious, the intemperate, would rush into the utmost extravagance of debauchery, sell and spend all their share, and then demand a new division of those who purchased from them. The moment the idea is admitted into society, that property is not as sacred as the laws of God, and that there is not a force of law and public justice to protect it, anarchy and tyranny commence. If "Thou shalt not covet," and "Thou shalt not steal," were not commandments of Heaven, they must be made inviolable precepts in every society, before it can be civilized or made free.[10]

The right to private property—that is, the fruits of an individual's physical and intellectual labor—was known to be a keystone to a free society's foundation. It is a natural right, protected by natural law. In this there was no divergence between the Federalists and Anti-Federalists.

Given the primacy of property rights, the Framers insisted that
certain safeguards must be incorporated in the Constitution to
protect against excessive government intrusion. Therefore, as part
of the Bill of Rights, the Fifth Amendment provides explicitly,
". . . nor shall private property be taken for public use without just
compensation."[11]

Referred to in legal circles as the "Takings Clause," this provision obligates the government to compensate the property owner
when the government takes private property for some putative
public good. However, much debate surrounds the issue of what
actually constitutes a "taking." Those who insist on the all-
encompassing power of government claim a taking occurs only
when the government physically seizes property. Those who, like
the Founders, extol the indispensable value of property rights
in preserving a civil society recognize that a taking occurs also
when the government—by an act of Congress, state legislature,
or administrative regulation—effectively destroys or substantially
diminishes the market value of private property. These "regulatory takings," as they are called, are often indistinguishable from
actual, physical takings. These types of governmental actions may
not constitute an actual physical appropriation of property. Instead, they impose significant restrictions on the owners' use of
the property. Consequently, the property owner can suffer severe
economic damages should the restriction prevent the economic
development or private use of the property.

Again, the Framers placed the highest importance on property
rights, which they sought to protect from the government they
were establishing. They would not have cared which branch of
the federal government confiscated private property or whether it
was confiscated outright or by way of diminished value or use. For

the Framers, private property was inviolable, protected expressly in the Fifth Amendment.

Today the Supreme Court, endlessly seeking ways to reinforce if not promote the growing powers of the federal government, and especially the extensive and growing tentacles of the administrative state, discounts both the nation's history and heritage. It has limited severely the factors that constitute a regulatory taking that justify compensating the property owner.[12]

The Court has issued a host of opinions addressing the application of the Takings Clause. In 1922, Associate Justice Oliver Wendell Holmes Jr. first recognized a regulatory taking in *Pennsylvania Coal v. Mahon*. He wrote, "[W]hile property may be regulated to a certain extent, if regulation goes too far it will be recognized as a taking."[13] The imprecise standard of "too far" has confounded subsequent courts, which have attempted to apply a jumbled mass of tests and factors to determine whether a taking has occurred.

The Court has said that in certain limited instances, a regulatory taking will be considered a taking for purposes of the Fifth Amendment and the owner will be awarded "just compensation." In cases where there is a deprivation of "all economically beneficial use" of a property, the Court has acknowledged that the Fifth Amendment mandates that the property owner be awarded just compensation. In these cases, the regulation has made the property completely worthless. For partial regulatory takings, instances where the regulation only partially affects the value of the property, the outcome is not so certain. In 1978, in *Penn Central Transp. Co. v. New York City*, the Court wrote that there is no "set formula" for determining whether a partial regulatory taking merits compensation, but there are "factors that have particular significance."[14] These factors include "the economic impact of the regulation, particularly the extent to which the regulation has interfered with distinct investment-backed expectations."[15]

In 1992, in *Lucas v. South Carolina Coastal Council*, even Associate Justice Antonin Scalia indicated that a regulation devaluing a property of 95 percent of its value may not constitute a taking and the property owner would not necessarily be eligible for compensation.[16] In 1993, in *Concrete Pipe and Prods. of Cal. v. Constr. Laborers Pension Trust for So. Cal.*, the Court held that the "mere diminution in the value of property, however serious, is insufficient to demonstrate a taking."[17] It is not enough for a property's value to decrease as a result of the regulation; the owner must pass some convoluted test to establish a regulatory taking. In 2005, in *Lingle v. Chevron U.S.A. Inc.*, the Court said it would also consider the "character of the governmental action . . . whether [the regulatory taking] amounts to a physical invasion or instead merely affects property interests 'through some public program.' "[18]

These tortured rationales and unnecessarily complex tests discount a seminal and underlying principle of property rights—that is, the right to own and control one's property is a natural, fundamental right that should receive the highest level of legal protection. The burden should not fall to the individual to justify the government intrusion as one that meets a series of complicated and incoherent tests to qualify as a taking. Rather, the burden should be on the government to justify the appropriation as one necessary for the public interest. Then the onus rests with the government to compensate the individual for the negative economic effect the burden places on the owner's property interest.

This is not to confuse the government's role in preserving private property rights under its police powers with a taking. Well before the adoption of our Constitution, it was understood that one neighbor did not have a right to interfere with the ownership and use of another neighbor's property. For example, a property owner upstream does not have a right to use his property in a way that pollutes a stream flowing through the land of a property owner downstream, thereby destroying or diminishing the value of the downstream property. As such, the government is exercising its authority to protect private property rights, which also serves the societal good, not expand its power to confiscate or control private property for some asserted governmental purpose.

In the late 1980s, President Ronald Reagan issued Executive Order 12630, requiring federal agencies to consider the "taking implications" when an agency promulgated new regulations.[19] The order "was needed to protect public funds by minimizing government intrusion upon private property rights and to budget for the payment of just compensation when such intrusions were inevitable."[20] Although a noble acknowledgment of the importance of property rights, Executive Order 12630 lacked any enforcement mechanisms, because it did not provide a cause of action. Consequently, property owners could not use the agency finding in proving their claim that federal government action was considered a taking.

It is indicative that so extensive is the government's taking practices that there is no reliable calculation on its aggregate costs to society—either its costs to property owners or the costs to government in those relatively limited cases in which it actually compensates property owners. Meanwhile, there is no question that regulatory takings are swelling as government itself swells.

The proposed amendment does a number of things. It acknowledges the crucial distinction between the government exercising its legitimate police powers to protect private property rights and its obligation to compensate property owners when government action—whether a statute, administrative regulation, or executive order—interferes with the ownership and use of private property for an asserted public interest. If the government action serves a public interest, then the public must assume responsibility for the cost and compensate the property owner who suffers a loss in excess of ten thousand dollars. The proposed amendment will force the government to make more extensive and comprehensive cost-benefit calculations when exercising its legal authority, given that the cost burden shifts from the individual to the government.

Moreover, the proposed amendment creates an expanded legal basis for private property owners to assert a constitutionally acknowledged and protected right. The notion that a taking must be physical, total, or near total to trigger a "just compensation" defies the Framers' intent and the Fifth Amendment's purpose. It also renders moot the convoluted precedents and ad hoc tests promulgated by the Supreme Court, and instead establishes a more stable and predictable legal environment for property owners and users.

Finally, the proposed amendment is not limited to takings by the federal government. It applies to all levels of government. While I acknowledge that the state legislatures themselves will undoubtedly determine the scope of this proposed amendment, or one similar in purpose, if and when they decide to appoint delegates to attend a convention, I would encourage them to control their own abuses of state citizens. When an individual's property is diminished or devalued by government action, the individual does not much care which level of government is responsible for violating his property rights. After all, the right to own property and use it was so important that *the states* themselves insisted on making the protection unambiguous by incorporating the Takings Clause in the Fifth Amendment.

CHAPTER NINE

An Amendment to Grant the States Authority to Directly Amend the Constitution

SECTION 1: The State Legislatures, whenever two-thirds shall deem it necessary, may adopt Amendments to the Constitution.

SECTION 2: Each State Legislature adopting said Amendments must adopt Amendments identical in subject and wording to the other State Legislatures.

SECTION 3: A six-year time limit is placed on the adoption of an Amendment, starting from the date said Amendment is adopted by the first State Legislature. Each State Legislature adopting said Amendment shall provide an exact copy of the adopted Amendment, along with an affidavit signed and dated by the Speaker of the State Legislature, to the Archivist of the United States within fifteen calendar days of its adoption.

SECTION 4: Upon adoption of an Amendment, a State Legislature may not rescind the Amendment or modify it during the
six-year period in which the Amendment is under consideration
by the several States' Legislatures.

AS DISCUSSED EARLIER, ARTICLE V of the Constitution sets
forth the two processes for amending the Constitution:

> The Congress, whenever two thirds of both Houses shall
> deem it necessary, shall propose Amendments to this Con-
> stitution, or, on the Application of the Legislatures of two
> thirds of the several States, shall call a Convention for pro-
> posing Amendments, which, in either Case, shall be valid to
> all Intents and Purposes, as Part of this Constitution, when
> ratified by the Legislatures of three fourths of the several
> States or by Conventions in three fourths thereof, as the
> one or the other Mode of Ratification may be proposed by
> the Congress. . . .[1]

As the text and history make clear, the amendment processes
are difficult. A supermajority of two-thirds of the members of both
houses of Congress is required to propose amendments, or two-
thirds of the state legislatures are required to call for a convention to amend the Constitution—which means thirty-four states.
Moreover, three-fourths of the states—or thirty-eight states—
must ratify the proposed amendments either by votes of the state
legislatures or state conventions for them to be incorporated into
the Constitution.

The level of complexity in the amendment processes was intentional. The Framers envisioned a clear and specific purpose for

the system of government they established. The Constitution was not meant to be a detailed list of laws and edicts to micromanage people's behavior. It was not meant to change with factional or majoritarian impulses. And it was not meant to serve the political expedients of a class of governing masterminds and their fanatical followers. The Constitution's authors intended it to serve as a steady, reliable, and not easily altered apparatus of governance built upon "unalienable" rights by which a huge, diverse, and vigorous society could successfully govern itself. The amendment processes were intended to elevate any matter addressed in a proposed amendment beyond the realm of day-to-day political issues.

In the 226 years since the 1787 Convention, there have been only twenty-seven amendments added to the Constitution, including the first ten amendments—the Bill of Rights. Those were ratified simultaneously on December 15, 1791. The small number of successful amendments, however, is not due to a lack of effort. Approximately 11,539 proposed amendments to the Constitution have been introduced in both houses of Congress between 1789 and January 2, 2013.[2]

However, as discussed at length in preceding chapters, we live in a post-constitutional period due to the Progressive movement's successful political counterrevolution. The Statists have constructed an all-powerful centralized federal government, unleashing endless social experiments in pursuit of utopian designs. The federal branches have used judicial review, congressional delegation, broad abuses of the Commerce and Takings clauses, and the power of the purse (taxing, spending, and borrowing), among other things, to commandeer the sovereignty of the states and the citizenry. Indeed, the states and the citizenry are now consumed by an elephantine array of federal laws, regulations, and rulings, which torment, coerce, obstruct, and sabotage the individual's autonomy. The states that gave the federal government life now live mostly at its behest.

In 1908, Woodrow Wilson made clear the plans he and others set in motion when he declared, "No doubt a great deal of nonsense has been talked about the inalienable rights of the individual, and a great deal that was mere vague sentiment and pleasing speculation has been put forward as fundamental principle."[3] Wilson added, "Living political constitutions must be Darwinian in structure and practice," meaning the federal government must be in a constant state of motion and evolution.[4] Consequently, the individual is without independent, God-given natural rights, which form the basis for America's founding. The Constitution's text and the Framers' intent are of no consequence—unless, of course, they can be said to justify if not compel the republic's self-mutilation. But Wilson conflates the nature of a healthy and dynamic civil society, where individuals are mostly free to pursue their interests, with what was to be the character of the federal government—a stable, predictable, and just governing institution, the purpose of which was the civil society's conservation. Wilson's prescription, and that of the Statists, empowers the federal government to extend its authority in ways large and small, devouring the very civil society it was established to safeguard. Unmoored from the Constitution, federal power becomes more centralized and concentrated, and increasingly difficult to define or proscribe.

The Tenth Amendment underscores generally and simply the division of authority between the federal and state governments:

The powers not delegated to the United States by the Constitution, nor prohibited by it to the States, are reserved to the States respectively, or to the people.[5]

The Constitution would not have been ratified had the Federalists refused to agree to the inclusion of this explicit recognition of state sovereignty, carried over from the Articles of Confederation, as part of a series of amendments—which would be adopted when the First Congress convened. It is a declaration of the indispensable role of the states in American life, which is loosely referred to as federalism.

The most successful rhetorical attack on federalism today involves past slavery and segregation. As I explained in *Liberty and Tyranny*, it is more complex than the Statists recount. "It is a misreading of history to singularly condemn federalism for slavery. While there is no debating or excusing that southern states sanctioned slavery, at times they did so with the help of the federal government. Moreover, there is also no questioning that other states, mostly in the North, instituted policies and laws not only prohibiting slavery within their own borders, but defying efforts by southern states *and* the federal government to enforce slavery in the South."[6] For example, "prior to the Civil War, and at the behest of the southern states, in 1793 and 1850 the federal Fugitive Slave Laws were enacted to force recalcitrant northern states to return escaped slaves to their southern owners. Many northern states resisted by passing personal liberty laws, which created legal obstacles to the deportation of slaves back to the South. In the 1842 *Prigg v. Pennsylvania* case, the federal Supreme Court ruled these laws unconstitutional, arguing that they sought to preempt federal law, although it added that the northern states were not required to affirmatively assist the southern state that sought the return of the escaped slaves. In 1857, the Court ruled in *Dred Scott v. Sandford* that no slaves or descendants of slaves could be U.S. citizens, and that Congress's Missouri Compromise of 1820, which prohibited slavery in much of the new territories, was unconstitutional, for it denied slave owners their personal property rights. . . . [N]ot until 1862 did the federal government abolish slavery in the District of Columbia, which was wholly controlled by federal authorities. . . ."[7]

The nation could not forever tolerate slavery. And it did not. Nonetheless, slavery was a contentious issue not only between the states, but also within the states—including in towns and counties in southern states. It was contentious not only between the federal government and the states, but within the federal government—as between Congress and the president, and between the elected branches and the Supreme Court. The same can be said of post–Civil War segregation, which was opposed by many states and practiced by others—and upheld in 1896 by the *federal* Supreme Court in *Plessy v. Ferguson*.[8]

Indeed, President Wilson, a leading Progressive and harsh critic of the Constitution and federalism, was a racist and segregationist. *Reason* magazine's Charles Paul Freund wrote that "Wilson allowed various officials to segregate the toilets, cafeterias, and work areas of their departments. One justification involved health: White government workers had to be protected from contagious diseases, especially venereal diseases, that racists imagined were being spread by blacks. In extreme cases, federal officials built separate structures to house black workers. Most black diplomats were replaced by whites; numerous black federal officials in the South were removed from their posts; the local Washington police force and fire department stopped hiring blacks. Wilson's own view, as he expressed it to intimates, was that federal segregation was an act of kindness. . . ."[9]

It is not possible to conduct a fulsome history of slavery and segregation in these pages. It must be underscored, however, that the oppression of African-Americans could never be compatible with a civil society and the principles set forth in the Declaration of Independence, as Abraham Lincoln explained. In 1858, during his campaign for the Senate, Lincoln declared: "In [the Founders'] enlightened belief, nothing stamped with the Divine image and likeness was sent into the world to be trodden on, and degraded, and imbruted by its fellows. They grasped not only the whole race of man then living, but they reached forward and seized upon the farthest posterity. They erected a beacon to guide their children and their children's children, and the countless myriads who should inhabit the earth in other ages. Wise statesman as they were, they knew the tendency of prosperity to breed tyrants, and so they established these great self-evident truths, that when in the distant future some man, some faction, some interest, should set up the doctrine that none but rich men, or none but white men, were entitled to life, liberty and the pursuit of happiness, their posterity might look up again to the Declaration of Independence and take courage to renew the battle which their fathers began—so that truth, and justice, and mercy, and all the humane and Christian virtues might not be extinguished from the land; so that no man would hereafter dare to limit and circumscribe the great principles on which the temple of liberty was being built. . . ."[10]

This brief and incomplete detour into this subject is necessitated by the anticipated hyperbole that frequently accompanies present-day discussions about, and efforts to, unravel and decentralize the federal Leviathan and reestablish federalism and republican governance—which is intended to uphold the sovereignty and dignity of the individual regardless of race, ethnicity, gender, age, ancestry, or station. In this regard, there is no denying that some states today are more amenable to personal and economic liberty than others. For example, the libertarian Mercatus Center at George Mason University measures "state and local government intervention across a wide range of public policies, from income taxation to gun control, from homeschooling regulation to drug policy." Its rankings "explicitly ground our conception of freedom on an individual-rights framework. In our view, individuals should be allowed to dispose of their lives, liberties, and properties as they see fit, as long as they do not infringe on the rights of others." For 2012, it ranked North Dakota, South Dakota, Tennessee, New Hampshire, and Oklahoma as the freest states, and New York, California, New Jersey, Hawaii, and Rhode Island at the bottom of the list.[11]

The struggle today, however, is not about the acknowledged burdens of any particular state, but between the continuing ascendency of Statist utopianism and restoring the governing principles of the American Republic. It should be understood that this proposed amendment is not intended as a reflection on the infallibility of state governments and their officials. The history of man is a history of human imperfection. In fact, the reason the Framers established checks, balances, enumerations, and divisions of power in the Constitution is that they understood, by knowledge and experience, that a relative handful of imperfect human beings exercising unrestrained authority over society would result in tyranny. But individuals can escape the burdens of a given state, for mobility is among the most important characteristics of federalism, as demonstrated by population growth and decreases in respective states. There is no escaping the reach of the federal government, however, unless the individual makes the difficult and wrenching decision to give up on the country altogether and leave for other shores.

Federalism also defuses conflict and even promotes harmony. Proponents of the death penalty can live in Texas, which has the most active execution chamber, and not care much that New Jersey abolished the punishment. Proponents of right-to-work laws can live in Virginia, and not care much that Pennsylvania is a union-friendly state. States are governmental entities that reflect the personalities, characteristics, histories, and priorities of the individuals who choose to inhabit them. They have diverse geographies, climates, resources, and populations. No two states are alike. States are more likely to better reflect the interests of their citizens—localities even more so—albeit imperfectly, than the federal government. Consequently, individuals with widely divergent beliefs are able to coexist in the same country because of the diversity and tolerance that federalism promotes.

It is undeniable that the states created the federal government and enumerated its powers among three separate branches; the states reserved for themselves all governing powers not granted to the federal government; and the Constitution they established enshrined both. *The Federalist Papers* emphasize this truism. In *Federalist* 39, James Madison argued that the federal government has only "certain enumerated" powers and the states retained "residuary and inviolable sovereignty" over all else. "Each State, independent of all others, and only to be bound by its own voluntary act. In this relation, then, the new Constitution will, if established, be a FEDERAL, and not a NATIONAL constitution."[12] In *Federalist* 45, Madison asserted that the proposed federal powers were "few and defined" and the power in the states remained "numerous and indefinite."[13] This was even before the adoption of the Tenth Amendment.

The ratification of the Constitution was, in fact, in doubt in certain large states, including Massachusetts, Virginia, and New York. The Federalists were forced to agree to introduce a number of amendments when the First Congress would meet after the Constitution's ratification. The purpose of the amendments was to further protect the individual from potential abuses by the new central government. It is important to recognize that it was several of the states, at the urging of the Anti-Federalists, which threatened to scuttle the ratification of the Constitution. They insisted on what would later become the Bill of Rights. The states were relied on by the citizenry to uphold their freedom and rights and serve as a buffer between the federal government and the individual.

For example, on February 6, 1788, the Massachusetts Ratification Convention not only ratified the Constitution, but in so doing set forth a number of proposed "amendments & alterations . . . that would remove the fears & quiet the apprehensions of many of the good people of this Commonwealth & more effectually guard against an undue administration of the Federal Government. . . ."[14] The Convention recommended, in part:

. . . That it be explicitly declared that all Powers not expressly delegated by the aforesaid Constitution are reserved to the several States to be by them exercised. . . .

. . . That no person shall be tried for any Crime by which he may incur an infamous punishment or loss of life until he be first indicted by a Grand Jury, except in such cases as may arise in the Government & regulation of the Land and Naval forces. . . .

. . . In civil actions between Citizens of different States every issue of fact arising in Actions at common law shall be tried by a Jury if the parties or either of them request it. . . .[15]

On June 27, 1788, the Virginia Ratification Convention ratified the Constitution but also proposed "[t]hat there be a Declaration or Bill of Rights asserting and securing from encroachment the essential and unalienable rights of the people."[16] Among the proposals:

. . . That there are certain natural rights of which men when they form a social compact cannot deprive or divest their posterity, among which are the enjoyment of life, and liberty, with the means of acquiring, possessing and protecting property, and pursuing and obtaining happiness and safety.

. . . That all power is naturally vested in, and consequently derived from, the people; that magistrates therefore are their trustees, and agents, and at all times amenable to them. . . .

. . . That in all criminal and capital prosecutions, a man hath a right to demand the cause and nature of his accusation, to be confronted with the accusers and witnesses, to call for evidence and be allowed counsel in his favor, and to a fair and speedy trial by an impartial jury of his vicinage, without whose unanimous consent he cannot be found guilty (except in the government of the land and naval forces) nor can he be compelled to give evidence against himself.

. . . That no freeman ought to be taken, imprisoned, or disseized of his freehold, liberties, privileges or franchises, or outlawed, or exiled, or in any manner destroyed or deprived of his life, liberty, or property, but by the law of the land.

. . . That every freeman restrained of his liberty is entitled to a remedy to enquire into the lawfulness thereof, and to remove the same, if unlawful, and that such remedy ought not to be denied nor delayed.

. . . That in controversies respecting property, and in suits between man and man, the ancient trial by jury, is one of the greatest securities to the rights of the people, and ought to remain sacred and inviolable. . . .

. . . That excessive bail ought not be required, nor excessive fines imposed, nor cruel and unusual punishment inflicted.

. . . That every freeman has a right to be secure from all unreasonable searches and seizures of his person, his papers, and property: all warrants therefore to search suspected places, or seize any freeman, his papers or property, without information upon oath (or affirmation of a person religiously scrupulous of taking an oath) of legal and sufficient cause, are grievous and oppressive, and all general warrants to search suspected places, or to apprehend any suspected person without specially naming or describing the place or person, are dangerous and ought not be granted.

. . . That people have a right peaceably to assemble together and consult for the common good, or to instruct their Representatives; and that every freeman has a right to petition or apply to the Legislature for redress of grievances.

... That the people have a right to freedom of speech, and of writing and publishing their sentiments; that the freedom of the press is one of the greatest bulwarks of liberty, and ought not to be violated.

... That the people have a right to keep and bear arms; that a well regulated militia composed of the body of the people trained to arms, is the proper, natural and safe defence of a free States.... [T]he military should be under strict subordination to the governed by the civil power.

... That no soldier in time of peace ought to be quartered in any house without the consent of the owners, and in time of war in such manner only as the laws direct.

... [A]ll men have an equal, natural and unalienable right to the free exercise of religion according to the dictates of conscience, and that no particular religious sect or society ought to be favored or established by law in preference to others.... [17]

On July 26, 1788, the New York Ratification Convention ratified the Constitution. However, it also forwarded a list of declarations, including:

... That the enjoyment of Life, Liberty and the pursuit of Happiness are essential rights which every Government ought to respect and preserve.

... [T]hat every Power, Jurisdiction and right, which is not by the said Constitution clearly delegated to the Congress of the United States, or the departments of the

Government thereof, remains to the People of the several States, or to their respective State Governments to whom they may have granted the same; And that those Clauses in the said Constitution, which declare, that Congress shall not have or exercise certain Powers, do not imply that Congress is entitled to any Powers not given by the said Constitution; but such Clauses are to be construed either as exceptions to certain specified Powers, or as inserted merely for greater Caution.

. . . That the People have an equal, natural and unalienable right, freely and peaceably, to Exercise their Religion according to the dictates of Conscience, and that no Religious Sect or Society ought to be favoured or established by Law in preference of others.

. . . That the People have a right to keep and bear Arms; that a well regulated Militia, including the body of the People capable of bearing Arms, is the proper, natural and safe defence of a free State . . .

. . . [T]hat at all times, the Military should be under strict Subordination to the civil Power.

. . . That in time of Peace no Soldier ought to be quartered in any House without the consent of the Owner, and in time of war only by the civil Magistrate in such manner as the Laws may direct.

. . . That no Person ought to be taken imprisoned, or disseised of his freehold, or be exiled or deprived of his Privileges, Franchises, Life, Liberty or Property, but by due process of Law.

. . . That no Person ought to be put twice in Jeopardy of Life or Limb for one and the same Offence, nor, unless in case of impeachment, be punished more than once for the same Offence.

. . . That every Person restrained of His Liberty is entitled to an enquiry into the lawfulness of such restraint, and to a removal thereof if unlawful, and that such enquiry and removal ought not to be denied or delayed, except when on account of Public Danger the Congress shall suspend the privilege of the Writ of Habeas Corpus.

. . . That excessive Bail ought not to be required; nor excessive Fines imposed; nor Cruel or unusual Punishments inflicted.

. . . That (except in the Government of the Land and Naval Forces, and of the Militia when in actual Service, and in cases of Impeachment) a Presentment of Indictment by a Grand Jury ought to be observed as a necessary preliminary to the trial of all Crimes cognizable by the Judiciary of the United States, and such Trial should be speedy, public, and by an impartial Jury of the County where the Crime was committed; and that no person can be found Guilty without the unanimous consent of Jury. . . . And that in all Criminal Prosecutions, the Accused ought to be informed of the cause and nature of his Accusation, to be confronted with his accusers and the Witness against him, to have the means of producing Witnesses, and the assistance of Council for his defense, and should not be compelled to give Evidence against himself.

. . . That the trial by Jury in the extent that it obtains by the Common Law of England is one of the greatest securities to the rights of a free People, and ought to remain inviolate.

. . . That every Freeman has a right to be secure from all unreasonable searches and seizures of his person, his paper

or his property, and therefore, that all Warrants to search
suspected places or seize any Freeman his papers or property,
without information upon Oath and Affirmation of sufficient cause, are grievous and oppressive; and that all general
Warrants (or such in which the place or person suspected
are not particularly designated) are dangerous and ought not
to be granted.

. . . That the People have a right peaceably to assemble together to consult for their common good, or to instruct their Representatives; and that every person has a
right to Petition or apply to the Legislature for redress of
Grievances.—That the Freeman of the Press ought not be
violated or restrained. . . .

. . . That the Jurisdiction of the Supreme Court of the
United States, or of any other Court to be instituted by
Congress, is not in any case to be increased enlarged or ex-
tended by any Fiction Collusion or mere suggestion;—And
That no Treaty is to be construed so to operate as to alter
the Constitution of any State. . . .[18]

Nonetheless, after the Constitution was ratified, and the First
Congress convened, the Federalists controlled both Houses, and
they were in no hurry to consider any amendments. Madison, a
member of the House from Virginia, continued pressing Congress to take up the matter, given the representations that had
been made to state ratification delegates, particularly the Anti-
Federalists.

On June 8, 1789, Madison was eventually able to raise the
subject of his proposed amendments, which were patterned after
those urged by several states. He had wanted the whole House to

take up the amendments. Instead, they would be submitted to a committee for consideration. Madison began his speech to the House this way: "I am sorry to be accessory to the loss of a single moment of time by the House. If I had been indulged in my motion, and we had gone into a Committee of the Whole, I think we might have rose and resumed the consideration of other business before this time; that is, so far as it depended upon what I proposed to bring forward. As that mode seems not to give satisfaction, I will withdraw the motion, and move you, sir, that a select committee to be appointed to consider and report such amendments as are proper for Congress to propose to the Legislatures of the several States. . . ."[19]

During the course of his speech, Madison noted that "there is a great probability that such a declaration (bill of rights) in the federal system would be enforced; because the State Legislatures will jealously and closely watch the operation of this [federal] government, and be able to resist with more effect every assumption of power than any other power on earth can do; and the greatest opponents to a federal government admit the State Legislatures to be sure guardians of the people's liberty. . . ."[20]

In *Ameritopia* I explained, "The debates between the Federalist and Anti-Federalist camps did not involve fundamental disagreements about the nature of man and inalienable rights, about which there was near-universal consent and for which a revolution had been fought and won, but how best to arrange a government, after the revolution, to ensure the perpetuation of American Society. The delegates at the constitutional and state conventions feared above all else the concentration of too much power in the new federal government. . . . Not only was there no support for an all-powerful central government, but the delegates

at the Constitutional Convention spent most of the summer trying to figure out how to ensure that no office or officeholder in
the new federal government would become too powerful. . . ."[21]

Moreover, the historical record is unequivocal, despite modern myths and misconceptions, that several of the states were the
impetus for the Constitution's recognition of, and emphasis on,
individual rights and autonomy vis-à-vis the federal government.

The proposed amendment is compelled because, among other
reasons, the Statists have achieved significant success in unraveling the Constitution and centralizing governmental power. As
I wrote in Liberty and Tyranny, "So distant is America today from
its founding principles that it is difficult to precisely describe the
nature of American government. It is not strictly a constitutional
republic, because the Constitution has been and continues to
be easily altered by a judicial oligarchy that mostly enforces, if
not expands, the Statist's agenda. It is not strictly a representative republic, because so many edicts are produced by a maze of
administrative departments that are unknown to the public and
detached from its sentiment. It is not strictly a federal republic,
because the states that gave the central government life now live
at its behest. What, then, is it? It is a society steadily transitioning
toward statism. . . ."[22]

As noted earlier, in Federalist 51, Madison wrote, in part, "But
what is government itself, but the greatest of all reflections on
human nature? If men were angels, no government would be necessary. If angels were to govern men, neither external nor internal
controls on government would be necessary. In framing a government which is to be administered by men over men, the great difficulty lies in this: you must first enable the government to control
the governed; and in the next place oblige it to control itself."[23]

To reiterate, no governing system is perfect. No level of government is perfect. This would seem obvious. Then why concentrate so much authority in the hands of so few imperfect individuals? And if men are incapable of managing their own affairs, what explains the ability of a relatively small number of them to manage the lives of so many others? The Framers knew the nature of man better than most, which is why they were careful and deliberate in establishing our constitutional system in the first place. But they also embraced the Enlightenment and its greatest architects, including John Locke and Charles de Montesquieu, as well as the Judeo-Christian spiritual emancipation of the individual, which preaches, among other things, man's altruism and capacity to improve and do good deeds.

The original constitutional construct—a social compact with limits, enumerations, divisions, etc.—was instituted to preserve the civil society and the individual's unalienable rights. But there is no denying that the federal government today is in many ways inimical to that purpose. The steady jog toward unbridled, centralized decision-making has become a sprint. The federal government has evolved into a colossus and the circle of liberty that surrounds each individual is shrinking.

The proposed amendment provides the body politic—that is, we, the people, through our state representatives, who live among us in our communities and with whom we can personally consult—with recourse against the federal government's usurpation of individual and state sovereignty. It assumes the citizenry rejects its growing subjugation by a class of governing masterminds who oversee an army of federal bureaucrats, and still de-

sire self-government and representation by consent. There is no
doubt this professional ruling class and its adherents, dug in for a
century or more and enjoying their dominance over society, will
object strenuously to any effort to rebalance the several governments and reestablish the Framers' aims, even though the federal
government will still retain considerable authority.

Furthermore, the proposed amendment, like the others, must
overcome a very difficult hurdle to even be considered by the
states—a process that has never been employed successfully in
the adoption and ratification of any of the existing twenty-seven
amendments. Again, Article V provides, in part: "[O]n the Application of the Legislatures of two thirds of the several States,
shall call a Convention for proposing Amendments, which, in
either Case, shall be valid to all Intents and Purposes, as Part
of this Constitution, when ratified by the Legislatures of three
fourths of the several States or by Conventions in three fourths
thereof. . . ."[24]

The proposed amendment would empower the states to by-
pass Congress altogether—that is, they would not be required to
make application to Congress in order to pursue amendments.
Even though making application to Congress is a ministerial
event, there is no persuasive reason the states need to adminis-
tratively organize their amendment efforts through Congress. In
fact, among the reasons the states may be moved to act is precisely
because of conflicts or disagreements with Congress. More importantly, the proposed amendment enables the states to amend
the Constitution directly, by a two-thirds (34) rather than three-
fourths (38) vote, and without convening a convention. This remains no easy task, given the political disparateness and other
diversities among the states. It is also a legitimate and lawful

means by which to amend the Constitution, although the hurdle remains high, unlike the frequent constitutional rewriting by federal officials that occurs today and has for decades.

In addition, the proposed amendment places a six-year limit on the time an amendment can be considered and adopted by the states, starting from the date it is first proposed by a sworn, certified filing by a state with the Archivist of the United States. Moreover, once a state ratifies a proposed amendment, the decision cannot be reversed and the proposed amendment cannot be modified during the six-year period. This prevents indecision, instability, and confusion in the state amendment process.

On June 6, 1788, during the Virginia Ratification Convention, Madison, responding to Patrick Henry's charge that the Constitution's enumerated powers would be usurped quickly by a federal government, asserted, "If the general government were wholly independent of the governments of the particular states, then, indeed, usurpation might be expected to the fullest extent. But, sir, on whom does this general government depend? It derives its authority from these governments, and from the same sources from which their authority derived. . . ."[25]

CHAPTER TEN

AN AMENDMENT TO
GRANT THE STATES AUTHORITY
TO CHECK CONGRESS

SECTION 1: There shall be a minimum of thirty days between the engrossing of a bill or resolution, including amendments, and its final passage by both Houses of Congress. During the engrossment period, the bill or resolution shall be placed on the public record, and there shall be no changes to the final bill or resolution.

SECTION 2: SECTION 1 may be overridden by two-thirds vote of the members of each House of Congress.

SECTION 3: Upon three-fifths vote of the state legislatures, the States may override a federal statute.

SECTION 4: Upon three-fifths vote of the state legislatures, the States may override Executive Branch regulations exceeding an economic burden of $100 million after said regulations have been finally approved by the Congressional Delegation Oversight Committee [see Chapter 9: An Amendment to Grant the States Authority to Directly Amend the Constitution].

SECTION 5: The States' override shall not be the subject of litigation or review in any Federal or State court, or oversight or interference by Congress or the President.

SECTION 6: The States' override authority must be exercised no later than twenty-four months from the date the President has signed the statute into law, or the Congressional Delegation Oversight Committee has approved a final regulation, after which the States are prohibited from exercising the override.

AS EXPLAINED EARLIER, THE level of complexity in amending the Constitution was intentional. However, in matters that require more timely redress and do not necessarily call for constitutional rebalancing, a more practical and, therefore, lesser threshold of three-fifths vote of the states (thirty states) would be appropriate. Moreover, unlike an amendment to the Constitution, the states would have the authority only to override specific federal laws or regulations, not replace them or modify them. Among other things, such a process would help relieve the intensifying dissatisfaction with congressional and bureaucratic interventions in the daily lives of the people. It would cause Congress to consider more seriously the reaction of the states and the consent of the people to the consequences of their lawmaking for fear that the states might override a bill or regulation. It would encourage and expand participation by the public in a democratic

and civil way, including working with state officials and organizing efforts at the local level, and serve as a counterweight to both
federal authoritarianism and street anarchy. And Congress would
be required to follow a constitutionally mandated discipline,
rather than abandon the deliberative process for "emergency"
legislation, and risk state override when adopting complex and
omnibus bills. In short, the proposed amendment would promote
a more rational legislative process in lieu of the current autocratic
disorder, and extend republicanism in contrast to its ongoing contraction.

In his *Commentaries on the Constitution of the United States*,
Associate Justice Joseph Story observed that "[a] government,
forever changing and changeable, is, indeed, in a state border-
ing upon anarchy and confusion. A government, which, in its
own organization, provides no means of change, but assumes to be
fixed and unalterable, must, after a while, become wholly unsuited
to the circumstances of the nation; and it will either degenerate
into a despotism, or by the pressure of its inequalities bring on a
revolution. It is wise, therefore, in every government, and especially in a republic, to provide means for altering, and improv-
ing the fabric of government, as time and experience, or the new
phases of human affairs, may render proper, to promote the happiness and safety of the people. The great principle to be sought is
to make the changes practicable, but not too easy; to secure due
deliberation, and caution; and to follow experience, rather than
to open a way for experiments, suggested by mere speculation or
theory."[1]

A primary purpose of the proposed amendment is to moderate and, at times, confine, if not undo, the tumult and perplexity
unleashed on society by hyperactive governing masterminds—

in this instance, Congress and its offspring, the administrative
state. Conversely, the proposed amendment promotes change
as reform, which is intended to preserve our founding principles
and restore our constitutional system. British statesman and philosopher Edmund Burke explained, "There is a manifest, marked
distinction, which ill men with ill designs, or weak men incapable of any design, will constantly be confounding,—that is, a
marked distinction between change and reformation. The former
alters the substance of the objects themselves, and gets rid of all
their essential good as well as of all the accidental evil annexed
to them. Change is novelty; and whether it is to operate any one
of the effects of reformation at all, or whether it may not contra-
dict the very principle upon which reformation is desired, cannot
be known beforehand. Reform is not change in the substance or
in the primary modification of the object, but a direct application of a remedy to the grievance complained of. So far as that
is removed, all is sure. It stops there; and if it fails, the substance
which underwent the operation, at the very worst, is but where
it was."[2]

Undue alterations and constant abstractions are the hallmarks
of the modern Congress and the administrative state. They are
especially notorious and deceitful, for they are often imposed in
the name of the people but without their consent or even knowledge. It is this exercise of arbitrary power, and the infliction of
social experiments by ambitious public officials—pushing and
pulling the individual from here to there, and tormenting him
nonstop by banning and mandating the most minute lifestyle
behaviors—which are intended to make subservient the individual's independence and unalienable rights. This is precisely what
the Constitution was crafted to blunt. There has never been a

compact for democratic tyranny in the United States. This clash of purposes—the clash of liberty and tyranny—goes to the heart of the matter and is the impetus for the proposed amendment.

On November 13, 1815, John Adams wrote Thomas Jefferson that "[t]he fundamental Article of my political Creed is, that Despotism, or unlimited Sovereignty, or absolute Power is the same in a Majority of a popular Assembly, an Aristocratical Counsel, an Oligarchical Junto and a single Emperor. Equally arbitrary cruel bloody and in every respect diabolical."[3] Provision is indispensable for greater input, not less, by the body politic in the conduct of national affairs, and in a manner consistent with constitutional republicanism. This is especially so today. The proposed amendment makes a necessity of cooperation, accommodation, and, more often than not, concurrence within the federal government, between the federal government and the states, and among the several states. It also creates opportunities for public inquiry and participation.

The additional federal and state legislative deliberations consequent to the proposed amendment's adoption would also slow the increasingly routine congressional practice of circumventing the subcommittee and committee hearing process for the sinister purpose of concealing the particulars of voluminous legislation, or rushed stopgap measures, even from rank-and-file lawmakers and the most attentive citizens. This a weak spot Thomas Jefferson raised in a letter to James Madison on December 20, 1787. Commenting on the Constitution adopted recently by the convention and awaiting ratification by the states, Jefferson warned of the "evil" of this kind of legislating. He wrote, "The instability of our laws is really an immense evil. I think it would be well to provide in our constitutions that there shall always be a twelvemonth between the ingrossing a bill and passing it: that it should then be offered to its passage without changing a word; and that if circumstances should be thought to require a speedier passage, it should take two thirds of both houses instead of a bare majority."[4]

More than two centuries after Jefferson's caution, on March 22, 2010, the House of Representatives barely passed the nearly three-thousand-page-long Obamacare law, by a margin of 219–212 (without a single Republican vote). As with the initial adoption of Social Security and Medicare, there was no great clamor for Obamacare. Moreover, the final version had not been made available to the public until shortly before it was voted on in the House. Consequently, its concealment prevented public scrutiny of its particulars. As then-Speaker Nancy Pelosi, just a few weeks prior to the vote, told the Legislative Conference for the National Association of Counties, "We have to pass the bill so that you can find out what is in it. . . ."[5] Since its passage more than three years ago, the people still do not know the full extent of Obamacare's effects. Meanwhile, thousands of pages of implementing regulations have been issued by the Department of Health and Human Services, the Internal Revenue Service, and other federal entities, imposing an untold number of mandates, controls, and costs on citizens.

So unpopular was the general proposition of Obamacare—namely, the unprecedented role the federal government would claim over individual health-care decisions—that even before the vote on the law, the House leadership was searching for ways to claim members had voted for it without members actually having done so—a stunning violation of the Constitution. In early March 2010, the House Rules Committee proposed a rule to the full House, aka the "Slaughter Rule," providing that, upon adoption of the House on a vote of yeas and nays of one bill (the "Reconciliation Bill"), an entirely different bill, H.R. 3590 (the "Senate Bill"), Obamacare would be "deemed approved" by the House. However, Article I, Section 7, Clause 2 of the Constitution states, "Every Bill which shall have passed the House of Representatives and the Senate, shall, before it becomes a Law, be presented to the President of the United States. . . ."[6] Thus, a law is enacted only if a bill containing its exact text is approved by a majority of the Members of the House; the Senate approves precisely the same text; and that text is signed into law by the president. Only after Landmark Legal Foundation threatened to sue the House for its planned subversion of the legislative process did the House leadership relent. Nonetheless, it is chilling that such a wholesale and blatant violation of the Constitution's lawmaking requirements came so close to execution.[7]

But the congressional goal was clear. As former president Bill Clinton insisted, "It's not important to be perfect here. It's important to act, to move, to start the ball rolling. There will be amendments to this effort, whatever they pass, next year and the year after and the year after, and there should be. It's a big, complicated, organic thing. But the worst thing to do is nothing."[8] In other words, it was important to install a massive health-care scheme as quickly as possible before the public could know what it was all about and there was a possible changeover in the congressional majority in the next election.

On July 21, 2010, a few months after adopting Obamacare, Congress passed the Dodd-Frank Wall Street Reform and Consumer Protection Act (Dodd-Frank). It was more than 2,300 pages long. During Congress's final negotiations, provisions were added to the bill with little debate and in many cases no hearings. Dodd-Frank requires four hundred separate rulemakings by eleven separate federal agencies.[9] It establishes the Consumer Financial Protection Bureau, which has unparalleled powers. It regulates credit and debit cards, mortgages, student loans, savings and checking accounts, and virtually every other consumer financial product and service. And the law actually attempts to immunize the bureau from oversight by future Congresses.[10] Two years after its passage, more than eight thousand pages of regulations had been issued, and regulators were only about 30 percent finished. Complying with the law is estimated to take about 24 million labor hours a year and require businesses to hire more than twenty-six thousand personnel just to comply with those already-finalized regulations.[11]

As of this writing, Congress is pursuing the same irresponsible and reckless course respecting so-called comprehensive immigration reform.

Moreover, when Congress is not violating its own budgetary law by passing continuing resolutions as emergency appropriation measures without public committee hearings, it is doing the opposite—that is, adopting massive spending bills that neither its members nor the public have had an opportunity to read. For example, in 2005, Congress passed the Deficit Reduction Omnibus Reconciliation Act, which was a combination of House and Senate bills that actually contained different and separate language. Its constitutionality was challenged in court, but the lawsuits were dismissed under the Enrollment Bill Rule, a practice whereby the courts concluded that the signed authentications by the president, Speaker of the House, and president of the Senate, and the formal printing of the bill, are incontrovertible proof that the law was passed validly.[12] Of course, this is a complete fiction. Each house of Congress is required to approve exactly the same legislation. Furthermore, omnibus bills are so extensive—thousands of pages in length involving scores of issues—that few know what is contained in them.

Recently, Congress passed the Violence Against Women Reauthorization Act of 2013 (VAWA).[13] Congress is in the habit of titling bills in such a way as to make difficult legitimate opposition to their adoption. The VAWA is such a bill. This law was passed in the Republican-controlled House with virtually no debate, and without the ability of a member to offer an amendment. Despite its title, the law is deeply flawed, as numerous commentators have noted, and raises serious doubts about its constitutionality in several respects, including the fundamental right to free speech and due process.[14] It also expands the definition of domestic violence to include "emotional distress" or the use of "unpleasant speech." It also grants more visas to illegal aliens who claim to be victims of domestic abuse.[15] In addition, this is a subject that both historically and constitutionally has been addressed at the state level. Even a cursory review of publicly available databases discloses that the states have passed numerous criminal statutes and instituted social service programs to help protect and care for abused individuals, and have done so for some time. This is not to say that a federal role, in certain circumstances, is illegitimate or unnecessary. But with the VAWA, Congress attempts to preempt and federalize most of the field and policy in this area. Back in 2000, in *United States v. Morrison*, the Supreme Court concluded that parts of the first Violence Against Women Act were unconstitutional, holding that the act exceeded congressional authority under the Commerce Clause and Fourteenth Amendment.[16]

Opposition to the law is not opposition to protecting victims of violence, but opposition to Congress's heavy hand in violating the Constitution.

These examples barely scratch the surface yet suffice in demonstrating the debacle of federal domineering, social engineering, and "expert" planning. When Congress passes immense and complex bills that virtually no one can comprehend, and often without constitutional power, and further delegates independent authority to the executive branch in violation of the separation-of-powers doctrine to pile regulations on top of laws—resulting in thousands of additional pages of rules—is this not the "Despotism, or unlimited Sovereignty, or absolute Power . . . [of] a Majority of a popular Assembly" of which John Adams warned?[17]

For all the talk by the governing masterminds about the commitment of more federal resources for education and the import of a well-informed people, the fact is that in their own legislative and regulatory quests and actions, opacity and obscurity are vital. The more distant from and less informed the public is about law-making and policy determinations, and their likely consequences on the individual and society generally, the less resistance and outright opposition can build against them. Enlightened public debate is to be avoided. Moreover, the will of the people can be said, albeit disingenuously, to be reflected in the actions of those for whom they voted—"the people get the government they deserve"—although the truth is otherwise, for the people know little of the actions taken by their members of Congress and still less of the regulatory maze engineered by the administrative state.

The colonists in pre–Revolutionary War America, having been taxed by the British without representation in the Parliament, used the slogan "No taxation without representation" to protest their lot. Today the rallying cry could be "No representation with representation." The point is that even though citizens vote for their members of Congress, members legislate in a manner that denies the people access to a transparent, orderly, and predictable lawmaking system, thereby avoiding true public scrutiny and input. Therefore, government decision-making becomes more centralized and power more concentrated. An insular ruling class intervenes arrogantly and boundlessly in the daily life of the individual, calibrating all nature of behavior. By no measure is such a contrivance representative republicanism. Edmund Burke explained it this way: "To them, the will, the wish, the want, the liberty, the toil, the blood of individuals is nothing. Individuality is left out of their scheme of government. The state is all in all. Everything is referred to the production of force; afterwards, everything is trusted to the use of it. It is military in its principle, in its maxims, in its spirit, and in all its movements. The state has dominion and conquest for its sole objects; dominion over minds by proselytism, over body by arms."[18]

This is a long way from the limits imposed on Congress by the Constitution, and its grant of specific and enumerated powers. The objective of the proposed amendment is, as I explained, to restore our founding prerogatives and discourage arbitrary and perplexing legislation and regulations, instituted by a growing, centralized decision-making regime hostile to constitutional constraints. It will encourage the expansion of actual republicanism and reverse federalism's steady dissolution. It will institute a truly deliberative and rational process within the federal government, between the federal government and the states, and among the states. And at all levels of deliberation, the citizen will have a genuine opportunity to participate in the governmental process, and hold his federal and state representatives politically accountable for their actions.

The proposed amendment requires a minimum of thirty days between the engrossing of a bill or resolution, including amendments, and its final passage by both houses of Congress. The purpose is to ensure that members of Congress, state officials, and the citizenry are aware of legislative actions before they become law. It also provides for speedier legislative action if agreed to by two-thirds of the members of each house of Congress.

In addition, the proposed amendment empowers the states, by a three-fifths supermajority vote, to override a federal statute or regulation (which regulation imposes an economic burden of $100 million or more), within a two-year period from the date of its legal implementation. The states cannot substitute their own alternative legislation for federal laws and regulations. Nor can they modify federal laws or regulations. The sole power of the states is to collectively override a law or regulation by three-fifths vote. Moreover, although the three-fifths vote is obviously a lesser threshold than the two-thirds requirement for amending the Constitution proposed in the previous amendment, it is still a challenging supermajority hurdle. For example, as demonstrated in the Obamacare litigation, at no time did the states suing to overturn the law reach thirty in number.

Clearly there is much political, social, and economic diversity among the states. Some states respect the individual more than others. Some are downright oppressive in their imposition of regulatory and tax schemes. But people can move from state to state, and often do, to escape one state's burdens for another state's opportunities. Federalism is not about any single state or small faction of states imposing their will on the nation. It is about states serving, in the aggregate, as an essential buffer between the central government and the people, safeguarding the citizen from authoritarianism's consolidated rule, thereby preserving and promoting self-government. After all, self-government is the fundamental feature of a constitutional republic. As Thomas Jefferson wrote, "It was by the sober sense of our citizens that we were safely and steadily conducted from monarchy to republicanism, and it is by the same agency alone we can be kept from falling back."[19]

CHAPTER ELEVEN

AN AMENDMENT TO
PROTECT THE VOTE

SECTION 1: Citizens in every state, territory, and the District of Columbia shall produce valid photographic identification documents demonstrating evidence of their citizenship, issued by the state government for the state in which the voter resides, as a requirement for registering to vote and voting in any primary or general election for President, Vice President, and members of Congress.

SECTION 2: Provisions shall be made by the state legislatures to provide such citizenship-designated photographic identification documents at no cost to individuals unable to afford fees associated with acquiring such documents.

SECTION 3: Early voting in any general election for President, Vice President, and members of Congress shall not be held more than thirty calendar days prior to the national day of election except for active-duty military personnel, for whom early voting shall not commence more than forty-five calendar days prior to the national day of election.

SECTION 4: Where registration and/or voting is not in person but by mail, citizens must submit an approved citizen-designated photo identification and other reliable information to state election officials to register to vote and request ballots for voting, no later than forty-five calendar days before the primary or general elections for President, Vice President, or members of Congress. Registration forms and ballots must be returned and signed by the voter and must either be mailed or hand-delivered by the voter to state election officials. If delivered by a third party, the voter must provide written authorization for the person making the delivery and the third party must sign a statement certifying that he did not unduly influence the voter's decisions.

SECTION 5: Electronic or other technology-based voting systems, for purposes of registering and voting in national elections, are proscribed unless a reliable identification and secure voting regimen is established by the state legislature.

ALTHOUGH THIS PROPOSED AMENDMENT does not involve systemic constitutional reform, as do the other proposed amendments, it addresses the sanctity of the voting franchise in federal elections, which has become increasingly confusing and unreliable. And like the other proposed amendments, this one is intended to enhance self-government.

The one mantra recited reflexively whenever the topic of voter fraud comes up is that there is no such thing as voter fraud in the United States. It just does not exist, so there is simply no need for "draconian" measures like requiring voters to present a state-issued photo identification—a valid driver's license, passport, or equivalent form of ID—in order to vote. Beyond a few "isolated" examples of individuals misbehaving, it is said that voter fraud does not occur.

This argument was addressed directly by Judge Richard Posner of the U.S. Court of Appeals for the Seventh Circuit in the 2008 *Crawford v. Marion County Election Board* decision, later upheld by the Supreme Court. Posner explained that we are dealing with ". . . the form of voting fraud in which a person shows up at the polls claiming to be someone else—someone who has left the district, or died, too recently to have been removed from the list of registered voters, or someone who has not voted yet on election day. Without requiring a photo ID, there is little if any chance of preventing this kind of fraud because busy poll workers are unlikely to scrutinize signatures carefully and argue with people who deny having forged someone else's signature."[1]

Posner added, ". . . the absence of prosecutions is explained by the endemic underenforcement of minor criminal laws (minor as they appear to the public and prosecutors, at all events) and by the extreme difficulty of apprehending a voter impersonator. He enters the polling place, gives a name that is not his own, votes, and leaves. If later it is discovered that the name he gave is that of a dead person, no one at the polling place will remember the face of the person who gave that name, and if someone did remember it, what would he do with the information?" He concluded,

"One response [to voting fraud], which has a parallel to littering, another crime the perpetrators of which are almost impossible to catch, would be to impose a very severe criminal penalty for voting fraud. Another, however, is to take preventive action . . . by requiring a photo ID."[2]

And what of the limited number of news reports of voter fraud? Posner pointed out, "[T]hat lacuna may reflect nothing more than the vagaries of journalists' and other investigators' choice of scandals to investigate."[3]

Incidents of in-person and other kinds of voter fraud also grow in complexity with each succeeding election cycle. Of course, there are conscientious citizens who try to ensure the integrity of our electoral infrastructure, but there are also self-interested political activists who are bent on adulterating the voting processes to the point where illicit activities like selling one's vote to the highest bidder, encouraging illegal aliens to register and vote—often multiple times in a single election—and tampering with absentee ballots are all too easily accomplished.

Not surprisingly, the catalysts for growing opportunities for electoral abuse are recently enacted federal laws designed to "reform" the processes by which we elect our leaders:

- Early voting—sometimes several days, weeks, and even months before election day.
- Same-day voter registration.
- Online voter registration.
- "Motor voter" registration (where an applicant for a new or renewed driver's license is automatically offered the opportunity to register to vote).

- Ballots published in non-English native and foreign languages.
- Provisional ballots.

While some of these measures have served to turn out new qualified voters, there have also been unadvertised consequences that are causing an increasing number of people to question the integrity of the voting process. And there is some talk of elections in the not-too-distant future taking place entirely online, with voters using smartphones, tablets, Internet-connected televisions, laptops, and desktop PCs to cast ballots.

This troubling electoral landscape has caused several states to enact, or consider enacting, statutes requiring voters to produce state-issued photo ID cards, primarily driver's licenses, as proof of citizenship to register to vote and vote in primaries and general elections. These laws are both eminently reasonable and very important tools in protecting the institutional credibility of the representative parts of government. Undermine the public's faith in the voting process, the single way in which the people can express directly their collective will, and you destabilize what is left of the republican enterprise.

And make no mistake, the public's faith has been shaken. According to an April 2012 Rasmussen poll, two out of three American voters surveyed believed that voter fraud is a serious problem. "Many think that people who should not be allowed to vote will actually be able to cast ballots," Rasmussen explained. The survey also found that 82 percent of those questioned believed that requiring a photo ID as a condition of voting was a good idea. And 73 percent rejected the notion that requiring a

photo ID would discriminate against minorities. Twenty-four percent of those surveyed also said that they were not confident that
their own vote would be counted.[4]

The Supreme Court has already weighed in on voter ID requirements, concluding they are a reasonable solution to voter integrity
concerns.[5] Regulations imposing only ordinary burdens, such as
those requiring a "nominal effort" by all voters, are not severe.

Several states are enacting laws requiring that voters present
one of several acceptable photo IDs. These laws are patterned
after an Indiana photo identification law that the Court has already upheld as a "generally applicable, nondiscriminatory voting
regulation" with reasonable burdens.[6]

Requiring a photo ID to vote is neither an onerous nor a
unique requirement in the twenty-first century. Identification
is required to obtain a driver's license and passport; buy alcohol
or cigarettes; apply for food stamps, unemployment, and various
forms of welfare; open a bank account; cash a check; purchase
a firearm; lease an apartment; rent a car; secure a marriage license; clear airport security; enter most federal buildings—and
even meet the president or vice president in person. Yet, when
it comes to state efforts to ensure the integrity of the electoral
process through modest voter identification laws, there are
howls of protest from certain political activists and insincere
public officials. Merely requiring an individual to establish eligibility for voting is portrayed as the resurrection of Jim Crow
laws.[7]

For example, Jesse Jackson declared, "The voter ID is the new
Civil War battle all over the nation."[8] Thus, for Jackson, identify-
ing yourself as a citizen before voting is akin to the war that ended

slavery. More troubling than Jackson's demagoguery is the deceitfulness of the nation's top law enforcement official. The attorney general of the United States, Eric Holder, used incendiary terms to critique the Texas voter ID law in a speech to the National Association for the Advancement of Colored People (NAACP): "Many of those without IDs would have to travel great distances to get them and some would struggle to pay for the documents they might need to obtain them. We call those poll taxes."[9]

Holder felt no urgency to offer any substantive information about exactly how many individuals would be inconvenienced by a photo ID requirement, or how those same individuals manage to function in their daily lives without a photo ID right now. Moreover, the irony was that the attendees of the speech had been asked to present identification before entering.[10] As attorney general, Holder should be more concerned than most about the integrity of the nation's voting system and the real and potential fraud that undermines it.

After a long history of civil rights struggles and legal battles to overcome real and intended sanctioned obstacles to voting, it would seem elemental that voting methodologies and processes that do not adequately protect the sanctity of the hard-won franchise warrant universal outrage. Extremist histrionics aside, many states are recognizing that the single most effective, straightforward, and practical way to discourage several types of voter fraud is to require a photo ID to establish identity. Unfortunately, in every state where this requirement has been enacted, opposition to these measures has been well organized, vitriolic, and dishonest. The contrived responses to recent reform efforts in Pennsylvania and Arizona are typical.

In Pennsylvania, the legislature concluded that the voters lacked confidence in the integrity of that commonwealth's electoral system. In 2012, it enacted a law requiring individuals to present a state-issued photo ID in order to vote.[11] Those without a photo ID would be issued a free ID by the state upon sufficient demonstration of identity and residency, which should have blunted complaints about affordability. Opposition to the bill was fierce, dominated by shameful claims of bigotry and racism, and efforts to create a false record of voter suppression.

Led by the American Civil Liberties Union and the NAACP, voter ID opponents claimed that the Pennsylvania law was intended to "suppress voting by groups that typically vote Democratic and disproportionately lack official ID."[12] They also claimed that the photo ID requirement is no different from a poll tax, now a common refrain. An NAACP attorney alleged that the Pennsylvania voter ID law was designed to disqualify "at the low end" 100,000 to 500,000 voters.[13]

Still, the legislature passed the bill, which the governor signed into law. Despite the alarmist rhetoric and brazen claims that hundreds of thousands of voters would be disenfranchised, the plaintiffs were unable to produce a single individual who would be prevented from voting under the new law.[14] A Pennsylvania trial court concluded that the voter ID law was a modest, generally applicable, nondiscriminatory adjustment to Pennsylvania's voter qualifications, fully consistent with the Pennsylvania Constitution.[15] After the intervention of the Pennsylvania Supreme Court, however, implementation of the law was delayed until after the 2012 presidential election. Administrative issues were the basis for delay rather than any substantive conclusion that the law is improper.[16]

In Arizona, voters amended the state's voter registration procedures by state initiative (Proposition 200) in 2004. Proposition 200 reflects the concerns Arizonans have in avoiding fraudulent voting by the large number of unqualified electors living within the state's borders. It requires county recorders to "reject any application for registration that is not accompanied by satisfactory evidence of United States citizenship."[17] Prospective registrants using the *federal voter registration form* mandated under the National Voter Registration Act are also required under Proposition 200 to provide one of various kinds of proof of citizenship in order to complete the registration since the federal form does not.

Since Arizona had been subject to federal supervision under the Voting Rights Act of 1965, the measure was submitted to the United States Department of Justice for approval, and became effective in January 2005.[18] As many as twenty thousand ineligible individuals were prevented from registering to vote during the year Proposition 200 was in effect.[19] The law served its purpose.

But opposition to Proposition 200 was incendiary and unrelenting. A lawsuit was initiated by numerous "civil rights" groups claiming that the measure discriminated against Native Americans, Hispanics, and other minority groups. The plaintiffs claimed the measure was a return to massive discrimination of the past and constituted a poll tax. A federal district judge threw out the case, concluding that the measure was a reasonable exercise of state sovereignty.[20] Eventually, the Ninth Circuit Court of Appeals ruled that while not constituting a poll tax or having any other discriminatory aspects, the Arizona law was preempted by a federal law that establishes standards for voter registration.[21]

Unfortunately, the Supreme Court ruled this June that

Arizona cannot require voter registration applicants to include evidence of citizenship when filing their *federal voter registration forms* (although applicants could choose to file the state form, which requires proof of citizenship, and which lawbreakers are obviously unlikely to do).[22] The 7 to 2 decision is another departure from explicit state authority recognized in the Constitution.

Article I, Section 2, Clause 1—the Constitution's Elector Qualifications Clause—could not be clearer. It provides, in part, ". . . the Electors in each State shall have the Qualifications requisite for Electors of the most numerous Branch of the State Legislature." Article I, Section 4 grants Congress authority to "make or alter such [state] Regulations" regarding "the Times, Places and Manner of holding Elections for Senators and Representatives." Therefore, Congress's power applies to how, when, and where to hold Elections—not about voter registration and voter qualifications. Moreover, as a secondary matter, Arizona's law did not conflict with the federal Motor Voter registration form. It improved upon it. The result is that the states are reduced to seeking approval from federal officials to do that which the Constitution already authorizes. Consequently, the Supreme Court permits states to require photo ID in order to vote, but disallows states from requiring photo ID or other forms of proof of citizenship as additional steps against fraud when registering with the federal registration form.

The modest, commonsense efforts by Pennsylvania and Arizona to ensure the integrity of the voter registration and voting process for all citizens have been replicated across the country. Legislatures in Kansas, Florida, Georgia, Indiana, Wisconsin, Missouri, Minnesota, Texas, and South Carolina, among others, are considering voting reform measures. In every case, opponents are employing racially and ethnically charged rhetoric to obstruct what should be noncontroversial measures, and are doing so often with the legal backing of the federal government.

It is worth noting that voting rights during the years of the Articles of Confederation, as they were during colonial times, were left strictly to the individual states. Most of the original states required men to be "freeholders"—landowners of either a minimum acreage or value.[23] Others required the payment of all taxes for the previous year.[24] Ten states had minimum residency requirements in the state or in a particular county.[25] Some states allowed "freemen" to vote while others allowed only white men to vote.[26] New Jersey was the only state that permitted women to vote.[27]

During the Constitutional Convention, the Framers weighed carefully the federal government's role in determining suffrage rights. They devised a system that was intended to preserve state sovereignty and ensure the viability of national elections in the Constitution. They ultimately designed a structure where members of the House of Representatives would be chosen directly by the people;[28] members of the Senate would be chosen by state legislatures;[29] and the president and vice president would be chosen by an Electoral College through a national popular vote.[30] Those voting in federal elections were to have the same qualifications as "Electors of the most numerous Branch of the [individual state's] State Legislature." This framework was a compromise between delegates to the Constitutional Convention who wanted all federal elected officials to be chosen by the States and those who argued for direct elections for all national offices.[31]

James Madison supported the compromise in *Federalist* 52, de-

spite his objections to it during the convention, arguing that the
Constitution's voting provisions

> appear, therefore, to be the best that lay within [the con-
> vention's] option. It must be satisfactory to every state be-
> cause it is conformable to the standard already established,
> or which may be established by the state itself. It will be safe
> to the United States; because being fixed by the state con-
> stitutions, it is not alterable by the state governments and it
> cannot be feared that the people of the state will alter this
> part of their constitutions, in such a manner as to abridge
> the rights secured to them by the federal constitution.[32]

During the state ratification conventions, several states proposed amendments requiring what amounted to a citizenship
requirement for voters. For example, the Virginia Ratification
Convention proposed "that the elections of representatives in the
legislature ought to be free and frequent, and *all men having sufficient evidence of permanent common interest with, and attachment
to the community*, ought to have the right of suffrage."[33] Rhode Island proposed the identical amendment.[34] Thomas Jefferson proposed to "include within the electorate of any county, along with
property holders, all free mail [sic] citizens who had resided there
for a year or had been enrolled that long in the militia."[35] These
were arguments for establishing standards that would require voters to have a stake in their communities.

Following the Constitution's ratification, some states dropped
property ownership and property tax payment requirements, but
most did not.[36] Over time, however, and as new states joined
the union, property ownership and taxation requirements were

dropped by most states. By 1855, only three of thirty-one states required property ownership or tax payments as a condition for voting.[37] But nearly every state required that voters be citizens or residents of the state for a minimum amount of time.[38] By the mid-1800s, only North Carolina allowed noncitizen voting.[39]

With the Civil Rights Act of 1964 and the Voting Rights Act of 1965 (VRA), Congress implemented measures that were intended to enforce the Thirteenth, Fourteenth, and Fifteenth Amendments—often referred to as the Civil War Amendments—to combat ingrained racial discrimination, particularly but not exclusively in certain Southern states. In addition to providing individuals with the right to sue when discriminated against, the federal government assumed sweeping "temporary" powers to eradicate racially discriminatory barriers to the ballot box, such as poll taxes and literacy tests.[40] The Department of Justice was given authority to preapprove all changes to voting laws for jurisdictions demonstrated to have institutionalized discriminatory laws.[41] This included everything from voter registration procedures to drawing district boundaries.[42] A five-year limit was put on this new federal authority because Congress and the judiciary recognized its shaky constitutionality respecting federalism and equal sovereignty among the states.[43]

In 1970, Congress renewed the "temporary" powers for another five years.[44] However, these powers were expanded to cover Hispanic, Asian, and Native Americans. The act was reauthorized for seven years in 1975 and for an additional twenty-five years in 1982. In the 1982 reauthorization, Congress expanded even further the act's scope by removing the requirement for intentional discrimination in certain voting cases.[45] The act was reauthorized for another twenty-five years in 2006.[46] While acknowledging that discriminatory practices existing in 1965 had been eradicated, Congress justified the 2006 reauthorization on the basis of "secondary barriers" to voting rights.[47] Consequently, with such an extensive federal role in overseeing voting in the nation, the resistance by federal officials to state efforts to actually ensure the integrity of the franchise—indeed, the federal government's legal actions and intimidation tactics in sabotaging and obstructing those efforts—was a profound desertion of self-government.

The original VRA had served its intended purpose, eradicating the evil of systematic race-based voter suppression. In another decision this June, the Supreme Court ruled that Congress could no longer justify the federal government's interference with state voting decisions based on conditions that had not existed for decades. It struck down the VRA's state preclearance requirements while preserving the individual's right to sue against alleged voter discrimination under the act.[48]

Meanwhile, two recent federal laws have contributed dramatically to creating the environment in which incidences of voter fraud can flourish—the National Voter Registration Act of 1993 and the Help America Vote Act of 2002 (HAVA).[49] Each of these laws has imposed requirements that restrict state authority to regulate elections and has opened the door for widespread abuses in both voter registration and voting at the polls.

In their book *Who's Counting? How Fraudsters and Bureaucrats Put Your Vote at Risk*,[50] election experts John Fund and Hans von Spakovsky supply numerous examples of pervasive problems in both the registration process and voter integrity throughout the nation. They fall into two broad categories—noncitizen voter registration and voting as well as voter fraud, combined with

the refusal of federal officials to enforce the law. Fund and von Spakovsky, among others, have demonstrated that aliens, both legal and illegal, are registering and voting in federal, state, and local elections. In fact, the federal government acknowledges it.[51] "There is no reliable method of determining the number of non-citizens registered, or actually voting, because most laws meant to ensure that only citizens vote are ignored, are inadequate, or are systematically undermined by government officials. Those who ignore the implications of noncitizen voting are willfully blind to the problem, or may actually approve of illegal voting."[52]

Noncitizens are on voter registration lists throughout the country. In 2005, the Government Accountability Office found that up to 3 percent of the thirty thousand individuals called for jury duty from voter registration rolls, during a two-year period in just one United States district court, were not citizens.[53] This particular district was in Florida, but Florida is not distinctive.

Colorado's secretary of state, Scott Gessler, is among a handful of state officials who have aggressively sought to enforce the HAVA. "The Colorado secretary of state testified before Congress in 2011 that a check of voter registration rolls against state [Division of Motor Vehicles] records indicated that more than 11,000 Colorado registered voters may not be U.S. citizens—and more than 5,000 of them voted."[54]

One of the many factors that may contribute to illegal aliens being able to register to vote is that there is no single voter registration system for the nation. There are fifty state (and the District of Columbia and U.S. territorial) systems operating at varying degrees of efficiency. And each of these systems depends on the skills, expertise, experience, and commitment of thousands of private citizens who man the polling places, operate the voting

machines, and count and report the tallies at the end of the day. Further complicating the situation are the various federal requirements overlaid on these state systems, creating a nearly perfect storm of inadequate resources, outdated equipment, and often un- or ill-trained volunteers running the systems on election day.

According to a 2012 analysis by the Pew Center on the States, there are more than 1.8 million deceased individuals who remain on voter registration rolls.[55] In addition, approximately 2.75 million people have registrations in more than one state.[56] Moreover, as many as 24 million—one in every eight—voter registrations in the United States are no longer valid or are significantly inaccurate.[57]

At least respecting the election of the president, vice president, and members of Congress, requiring a state-issued form of identification proving citizenship can be the foundation for reforming voting mechanisms, while preserving the roles of the federal and state governments in the process.

Ensuring the integrity of the voting process is a rational and essential objective. In fact, the Framers believed that there was a common responsibility, a unique symbiosis, between the federal and state governments in the *administration of elections*. Again, Article I, Section 4, Clause 1 provides, "The times, Places and Manner of holding Elections for Senators and Representatives, shall be prescribed in each State by the Legislature thereof; but the Congress may at any time by Law make or alter such Regulations, except as to the Places for chusing [sic] Senators."[58]

The Framers also granted the state legislatures the authority to determine how members of the Electoral College would be selected in their state. "Each State shall appoint, in such Manner as

the Legislature thereof may direct, a Number of Electors, equal to the whole Number of Senators and Representatives to which the State may be entitled in the Congress: but no Senator or Representative, or Person holding an Office of Trust or Profit under the United States, shall be appointed an Elector." [59]

Shortly after ensuring that the state legislatures would set the terms of selecting electors, Congress was granted a share of the responsibility for conducting presidential elections. "The Congress may determine the Time of chusing the Electors, and the Day on which they shall give their Votes; which day shall be the same throughout the United States." [60]

Furthermore, there are four constitutional amendments that break down legal obstacles to voting and expand the franchise—all of which, of course, required ratification by three-fourths of the states after their adoption by two-thirds of both houses of Congress.

The Fifteenth Amendment ensures the right of former slaves to vote: "The right of citizens of the United States to vote shall not be denied or abridged by the United States or by any State on account of race, color, or previous condition of servitude." [61]

The Nineteenth Amendment ensures that women can vote: "The right of citizens of the United States to vote shall not be denied or abridged by the United States or by any State on account of sex." [62]

The Twenty-Fourth Amendment eliminates the poll tax, used by segregationists to prevent poor minorities, mostly African-Americans, from voting: "The right of citizens of the United States in any primary or other election for President or Vice President, for electors for President or Vice President, or for Senator

or Representative in Congress, shall not be denied or abridged by the United States or any State by reason of failure to pay any poll tax or other tax."[63]

Lastly, the Twenty-Sixth Amendment reduces the age of eligibility to vote. "The right of citizens of the United States, who are eighteen years of age or older, to vote shall not be denied or abridged by the United States or by any State on account of age."[64]

The proposed amendment is intended to ensure that the franchise is secure for all citizens. First, it establishes the requirement for producing an official photo ID that designates the individual's citizenship to register to vote and vote. Although it is conceivable that a particular individual might not be able to satisfy a photo ID requirement, such IDs would be provided free of charge, as provided in every state that has adopted the photo ID requirement.

Moreover, the proposed amendment continues early voting, but only when circumstances warrant and only for a limited, specified time period, contrary to the chaotic trend toward multi-month-long voting cycles. As with most laws, the election laws—at least respecting the selection of the president, vice president, and members of Congress—need to be predictable, reliable, and consistent.

Indeed, limiting the number of early-voting days will ensure that the electorate will be casting their votes under the same general conditions. The advent of earlier and earlier voting schemes has produced circumstances where the electorate is divided into segments of dissimilarly informed voters. Some vot-

ers are making their judgments shortly after primary elections, others just before or after national party conventions, and still more following one or more candidate debates. The remaining electorate casts its ballots after a fully completed campaign. Premature decisions can lead to perverse results. The objective of federal elections is to achieve a national judgment for national leadership.

Furthermore, under the proposed amendment, where registration and/or voting is not in person, such as by mail, voters must submit an approved citizen-designated photo ID demonstrating eligibility for voting to become registered to vote and request ballots from state election officials no later than forty-five calendar days before the primary or general elections. And to ensure mail-in ballot security, ballots must also be returned and signed by the voter and must either be mailed or hand-delivered by the voter to election officials. If delivered by a third party, the voter must provide written authorization for the person making the delivery and the third party must sign a statement certifying that he did not unduly influence the voter's decisions.

Finally, no state may adopt an electronic voting system (or other technology-based systems) unless it is reliably secure, given the vulnerability of electronic databases to cyberattacks and other forms of hacking, manipulation, and corruption.

The proposed amendment's language and purpose are straightforward. The voter registration and voting requirements are vastly less burdensome and complicated than, for example, the Internal Revenue Code, Obamacare, Dodd-Frank, and most federal laws and regulations that engulf a citizen in his daily life. The proposed amendment will improve the integrity and reliability of the electoral process in national elections, which is increasingly chaotic; deter and detect voter fraud; and ensure that only individuals who are entitled to vote—citizens—actually vote. The proposed amendment is neutral, nondiscriminatory, and champions universal suffrage.

EPILOGUE

THE TIME FOR ACTION

No DOUBT, IN A twist of logic, the state convention process and *The Liberty Amendments* will be assaulted by the governing masterminds and their disciples as an extreme departure from the status quo and, therefore, heretical, as they resist ferociously all efforts to diminish their power and position. Paradoxically, it is they who distort the Constitution's text and trespass its purpose by actively pursuing its nullification and abandonment. History demonstrates that republics collapse when demagogues present themselves as their guardians to entice the people and cloak their true intentions. I have no illusions about the Statists' capacity to induce confusion and spread disinformation in defense of their own ambition and aggrandizement. Indeed, the closer the approach to constitutional restoration, should that day arrive, a torrent of fuming and malevolent rage will, predictably, let loose, alleging perfidy by the true reformers.

Moreover, it is an obtuse and defeatist notion of moderation that accepts the disposition of inevitable societal self-destruction without recourse to an available escape. Its irrationality is self-evident. Reacquainting ourselves with a legitimate constitutional remedy, which we, the people, cherish and our public officials swear to uphold, should not be perceived or dismissed as a radical deviation from normative principles but a prudent, rational, and civil response to their disembowelment. The state convention process is a product of the Constitutional Convention, envisioned for exactly this moment, and *The Liberty Amendments* are intended to restore the Framers' work. This is not to say that all class of doubters, holding contrary sentiments, should be dismissed and their arguments declared meritless or contrived. Rational debate stimulates improvement by tapping into the experience, knowledge, and judgment of others. The entire state convention enterprise relies on, and rouses, the broadest public participation and deliberation.

There will also be those who insist sincerely that electing the right president and Congress, and appointing the right justices, is not only more practicable but preferable to amending the Constitution. They will cling to a particular election or judicial decision as evidence of vibrant republicanism, deluded by short respites and interludes to escape the intellectual and practical reality of societal transformation. I am all for the election of candidates and the confirmation of justices who are faithful to the Constitution. Obviously, the amendment process does not preclude such efforts. But let us acknowledge the infrequency of these occurrences and the greater rarity of fidelity by these officials, once ensconced in high office, to constitutional boundaries. In fact, even the most virtuous and resourceful among them do not and cannot possess the aptitude and muscle to penetrate the daunting entrenchment and institutionalized apparatuses of the federal government. Furthermore, the increasingly and significantly cloistered operations of the federal branches, the willful concealment of deliberations, the delegation of power to elusive and unaccountable bureaucracies, and the centralization and concentration of authority are all intended to evade the Constitution, confound the citizen, and suppress self-government. This is a systemic problem that is bigger than any single federal election or administration.

The unambiguous evidence reveals that much of what the federal government does is unaffected by elections; this is the consequence of the Statists' design. Like Woodrow Wilson several years before him, Franklin Roosevelt made public his frustration and conceit, doing so on May 18, 1926, in a lecture at Milton Academy titled "Whither Bound?" Roosevelt lamented the limits of constitutional republicanism on the federal government's power.[1] As he explained, "Measured by years the actual control of human affairs is in the hands of conservatives for longer periods than in those of liberals or radicals. When the latter do come into power, they translate the constantly working leaven of progress into law or custom or use, but rarely obtain enough time in control to make further economic or social experiments. . . . Our national danger is, however, not that it may for four years or eight years become liberal or even radical, but that it may suffer from too long a period of the do-nothing or reactionary standards."[2]

Thus, upon ascending to the presidency, Roosevelt erected an autocratic program to overcome the transience of Statist electoral victories and interrupted rule, about which he had earlier complained. Roosevelt altered the character of our constitutional system and mounted a lasting policy agenda largely invulnerable to opposition electoral victories and legal challenges. The repercussions were never in doubt and are now ever more tangible, with a definite upshot—devouring the civil society and subsuming individual sovereignty. This is precisely why the Framers provided in Article V a backstop to restore constitutional republicanism.

Meanwhile, the American people are extremely dissatisfied with the federal government. Nearly three-fourths view it unfavorably; only 28 percent favorably. Conversely, local and state governments are regarded more highly by large majorities, 63 percent and 57 percent, respectively.[3] This creates an extremely volatile and unhealthy atmosphere in what is supposed to be a "government of the people, by the people, and for the people."[4] How much longer can such widespread and deep public discontent with the federal government persist? Is it not time to rescue what is ours by civil and legitimate means?

The state legislatures, acting collectively, have enormous power. They grasp the ultimate authority to restore the American Republic and bolster the civil society. The state convention process bypasses the intractable architects of this calamity, who have obstructed and sabotaged all other routes to constitutional adherence. It is a bottom-up, grassroots initiative that empowers the citizenry, organizing in neighborhoods and communities, and working through the state legislatures, to stem federal domination, reverse course, and escape ruin.

The Framers, including George Mason, James Madison, and Alexander Hamilton, were not alone in their support for the state convention process. As attorney Russell L. Caplan, in his book *Constitutional Brinkmanship*, notes, former president Dwight Eisenhower, during his commencement address in May 1963 at Defiance College in Ohio, urged the graduating class to help return the rights lost to "a distant bureaucracy." Eisenhower, also fed up with the Warren Court, stated, "Through their state legislatures and without regard to the federal government, the people can demand and participate in constitutional conventions in which they can, through their own action, adopt such amendments as can and will reverse any trends they see as fatal to true representative government."[5]

During his presidency, Ronald Reagan referred repeatedly and approvingly to the state convention process in his battles with Congress over federal spending, a balanced budget, and the budget process. On August 12, 1987, in a nationally televised speech from the Oval Office, Reagan stated, among other things, that "[t]he Congressional budget process is neither reliable nor credible—in short, it needs to be fixed. We desperately need the power of a constitutional amendment to help us balance the budget. Over 70 percent of the American people want such an amendment. They want the federal government to have what 44 state governments already have—discipline. If the Congress continues to oppose the wishes of the people by avoiding a vote on our balanced-budget amendment, the call for a constitutional convention will grow louder. . . ."[6]

The state convention process provides a constitutional way out, where, as George Mason declared, "the [federal] Government should become oppressive." And The Liberty Amendments offer a collection of reforms—a plan based on our founding principles—which address the Statists' most severe malpractices and distortions by decentralizing the accumulation of federal power, reviving federalism, and securing consensual governance.

I recognize the daunting task before us. But if there are better alternatives for effectively restoring the American Republic consistent with constitutional republicanism, not abstractions or novelties, they have hitherto not been presented. Perhaps, at a minimum, this project will kindle them. Let us hope so. There is no reason to be passive witnesses to societal dissolution, at the command of governing masterminds in the federal government and their disciples.

In the end, the people, upon reflection, will decide their own fate once their attention is drawn. As President Reagan stated, "You and I have a rendezvous with destiny. We will preserve for our children this, the last best hope of man on earth, or we will sentence them to take the first step into a thousand years of darkness. If we fail, at least let our children and our children's children say of us that we justified our brief moment here. We did all that could be done."[7]

Let us do all that can be done. Let us be inspired by the example of our forefathers and their courage, strength, and wisdom. Let us be inspirited by the genius of the Constitution and its preservation of the individual and the civil society. Let us unleash an American renaissance in which liberty is celebrated and self-government is cherished. Let us, together—*we, the people*—restore the splendor of the American Republic.

Time is of the essence. Let us get started today!

THE AMENDMENTS

An Amendment to Establish
Term Limits for Members of Congress

SECTION 1: No person may serve more than twelve years as a member of Congress, whether such service is exclusively in the House or the Senate or combined in both Houses.

SECTION 2: Upon ratification of this Article, any incumbent member of Congress whose term exceeds the twelve-year limit shall complete the current term, but thereafter shall be ineligible for further service as a member of Congress.

An Amendment to Restore the Senate

SECTION 1: The Seventeenth Amendment is hereby repealed. All Senators shall be chosen by their state legislatures as prescribed by Article I.

SECTION 2: This amendment shall not be so construed as to affect the term of any Senator chosen before it becomes valid as part of the Constitution.

SECTION 3: When vacancies occur in the representation of any State in the Senate for more than ninety days the governor of the State shall appoint an individual to fill the vacancy for the remainder of the term.

SECTION 4: A Senator may be removed from office by a two-thirds vote of the state legislature.

An Amendment to Establish Term Limits for Supreme Court Justices and Super-Majority Legislative Override

SECTION 1: No person may serve as Chief Justice or Associate Justice of the Supreme Court for more than a combined total of twelve years.

SECTION 2: Immediately upon ratification of this Amendment, Congress will organize the justices of the Supreme Court as equally as possible into three classes, with the justices assigned to each class in reverse seniority order, with the most senior justices in the earliest classes. The terms of office for the justices in the First Class will expire at the end of the fourth Year following the ratification of this Amendment, the terms for the justices of the Second Class will expire at the end of the eighth Year, and of the Third Class at the end of the twelfth Year, so that one-third of the justices may be chosen every fourth Year.

SECTION 3: When a vacancy occurs in the Supreme Court, the President shall nominate a new justice who, with the approval of a majority of the Senate, shall serve the remainder of the unexpired term. Justices who fill a vacancy for longer than half of an unexpired term may not be renominated to a full term.

SECTION 4: Upon three-fifths vote of the House of Representatives and the Senate, Congress may override a majority opinion rendered by the Supreme Court.

SECTION 5: The Congressional override under Section 4 is not subject to a Presidential veto and shall not be the subject of litigation or review in any Federal or State court.

SECTION 6: Upon three-fifths vote of the several state legislatures, the States may override a majority opinion rendered by the Supreme Court.

SECTION 7: The States' override under Section 6 shall not be the subject of litigation or review in any Federal or State court, or oversight or interference by Congress or the President.

SECTION 8: Congressional or State override authority under Sections 4 and 6 must be exercised no later than twenty-four months from the date of the Supreme Court rendering its majority opinion, after which date Congress and the States are prohibited from exercising the override.

Two Amendments to Limit
Federal Spending and Taxing

Spending

SECTION 1: Congress shall adopt a preliminary fiscal year budget no later than the first Monday in May for the following fiscal year, and submit said budget to the President for consideration.

SECTION 2: Shall Congress fail to adopt a final fiscal year budget prior to the start of each fiscal year, which shall commence on October 1 of each year, and shall the President fail to sign said budget into law, an automatic, across-the-board, 5 percent reduction in expenditures from the prior year's fiscal budget shall be imposed for the fiscal year in which a budget has not been adopted.

SECTION 3: Total outlays of the federal government for any fiscal year shall not exceed its receipts for that fiscal year.

SECTION 4: Total outlays of the federal government for each fiscal year shall not exceed 17.5 percent of the Nation's gross domestic product for the previous calendar year.

SECTION 5: Total receipts shall include all receipts of the United States Government but shall not include those derived from borrowing. Total outlays shall include all outlays of the United States Government except those for the repayment of debt principal.

SECTION 6: Congress may provide for a one-year suspension of one or more of the preceding sections in this Article by a three-fifths vote of both Houses of Congress, provided the vote is conducted by roll call and sets forth the specific excess of outlays over receipts or outlays over 17.5 percent of the Nation's gross domestic product.

SECTION 7: The limit on the debt of the United States held by the public shall not be increased unless three-fifths of both Houses of Congress shall provide for such an increase by roll call vote.

SECTION 8: This Amendment shall take effect in the fourth fiscal year after its ratification.

Taxing

SECTION 1: Congress shall not collect more than 15 percent of a person's annual income, from whatever source derived. "Person" shall include natural and legal persons.

SECTION 2: The deadline for filing federal income tax returns shall be the day before the date set for elections to federal office.

SECTION 3: Congress shall not collect tax on a decedent's estate.

SECTION 4: Congress shall not institute a value-added tax or national sales tax or any other tax in kind or form.

SECTION 5: This Amendment shall take effect in the fourth fiscal year after its ratification.

An Amendment to Limit the Federal Bureaucracy

SECTION 1: All federal departments and agencies shall expire if said departments and agencies are not individually reauthorized in stand-alone reauthorization bills every three years by a majority vote of the House of Representatives and the Senate.

SECTION 2: All Executive Branch regulations exceeding an economic burden of $100 million, as determined jointly by the Government Accountability Office and the Congressional Budget Office, shall be submitted to a permanent Joint Committee of Congress, hereafter the Congressional Delegation Oversight Committee, for review and approval prior to their implementation.

SECTION 3: The Committee shall consist of seven members of the House of Representatives, four chosen by the Speaker and three chosen by the Minority Leader; and seven members of the Senate, four chosen by the Majority Leader and three chosen by the Minority Leader. No member shall serve on the Committee beyond a single three-year term.

SECTION 4: The Committee shall vote no later than six months from the date of the submission of the regulation to the Committee. The Committee shall make no change to the regulation, either approving or disapproving the regulation by majority vote as submitted.

SECTION 5: If the Committee does not act within six months from the date of the submission of the regulation to the Committee, the regulation shall be considered disapproved and must not be implemented by the Executive Branch.

An Amendment to Promote Free Enterprise

SECTION 1: Congress's power to regulate Commerce is not a plenary grant of power to the federal government to regulate and control economic activity but a specific grant of power limited to preventing states from impeding commerce and trade between and among the several States.

SECTION 2: Congress's power to regulate Commerce does not extend to activity within a state, whether or not it affects interstate commerce; nor does it extend to compelling an individual or entity to participate in commerce or trade.

An Amendment to Protect Private Property

SECTION 1: When any governmental entity acts not to secure a private property right against actions that injure property owners, but to take property for a public use from a property owner by actual seizure or through regulation, which taking results in a market value reduction of the property, interference with the use of the property, or a financial loss to the property owner exceeding $10,000, the government shall compensate fully said property owner for such losses.

An Amendment to Grant the States
Authority to Directly Amend the Constitution

SECTION 1: The State Legislatures, whenever two-thirds shall deem it necessary, may adopt Amendments to the Constitution.

SECTION 2: Each State Legislature adopting said Amendments must adopt Amendments identical in subject and wording to the other State Legislatures.

SECTION 3: A six-year time limit is placed on the adoption of an Amendment, starting from the date said Amendment is adopted by the first State Legislature. Each State Legislature adopting said Amendment shall provide an exact copy of the adopted Amendment, along with an affidavit signed and dated by the Speaker of the State Legislature, to the Archivist of the United States within fifteen calendar days of its adoption.

SECTION 4: Upon adoption of an Amendment, a State Legislature may not rescind the Amendment or modify it during the six-year period in which the Amendment is under consideration by the several States' Legislatures.

An Amendment to Grant the States
Authority to Check Congress

SECTION 1: There shall be a minimum of thirty days between the engrossing of a bill or resolution, including amendments, and

its final passage by both Houses of Congress. During the engrossment period, the bill or resolution shall be placed on the public
record, and there shall be no changes to the final bill or resolution.

SECTION 2: SECTION 1 may be overridden by two-thirds vote
of the members of each House of Congress.

SECTION 3: Upon three-fifths vote of the state legislatures, the
States may override a federal statute.

SECTION 4: Upon three-fifths vote of the state legislatures,
the States may override Executive Branch regulations exceeding
an economic burden of $100 million after said regulations have
been finally approved by the Congressional Delegation Oversight
Committee [see An Amendment Establishing How the States
May Amend the Constitution].

SECTION 5: The States' override shall not be the subject of litigation or review in any Federal or State court, or oversight or interference by Congress or the President.

SECTION 6: The States' override authority must be exercised
no later than twenty-four months from the date the President
has signed the statute into law, or the Congressional Delegation
Oversight Committee has approved a final regulation, after which
the States are prohibited from exercising the override.

An Amendment to Protect the Vote

SECTION 1: Citizens in every state, territory, and the District of Columbia shall produce valid photographic identification documents demonstrating evidence of their citizenship, issued by the state government for the state in which the voter resides, as a prerequisite for registering to vote and voting in any primary or general election for President, Vice President, and members of Congress.

SECTION 2: Provisions shall be made by the state legislatures to provide such citizenship-designated photographic identification documents at no cost to individuals unable to afford fees associated with acquiring such documents.

SECTION 3: Early voting in any general election for President, Vice President, and members of Congress shall not be held more than thirty calendar days prior to the national day of election except for active-duty military personnel, for whom early voting shall not commence more than forty-five calendar days prior to the national day of election.

SECTION 4: Where registration and/or voting is not in person but by mail, citizens must submit an approved citizen-designated photo identification and other reliable information to state election officials to register to vote and request ballots for voting, no later than forty-five calendar days before the primary or general elections for President, Vice President, or members of Congress. Registration forms and ballots must be returned and signed by the voter and must either be mailed or hand-delivered by the voter to state election officials. If delivered by a third party, the voter must provide written authorization for the person making the delivery and the third party must sign a statement certifying that he did not unduly influence the voter's decisions.

SECTION 5: Electronic or other technology-based voting systems, for purposes of registering and voting in national elections, are proscribed unless a reliable identification and secure voting regimen is established by the state legislature.

ACKNOWLEDGMENTS

I am blessed and grateful for the love and support of my wonderful family. They are my greatest inspiration and encouragement, and always have been.

Thank you to Eric Christensen, Richard Hutchison, Michael O'Neill, and Matthew Forys, my colleagues and friends, for their excellent insights and research assistance; Mitchell Ivers, my longtime editor, for his superb advice; and my publisher, Louise Burke, for her steadfast support.

I also want to thank my treasured radio audience and the untold numbers of my fellow citizens who are committed, in small ways and large, to the restoration of the grand American Republic. We live in perilous times and the challenges are daunting. Yet we find strength and courage in our common bond as Americans. This is our generation's burden. We have our work cut out for us. But there is a way forward. The Constitution.

NOTES

1. Restoring the American Republic

1 Alexis de Tocqueville, *Democracy in America*, Henry Reeve, trans., Phillips Bradley, ed., vol. 1 (New York: Library of America, 2004), 319.

2 Ibid., 329.

3 "Obama: We are 5 days away from FUNDAMENTALLy [*sic*] transforming America," uploaded Oct. 31, 2008, http://www.you tube.com/watch?v=_cqN4NIEtOY (April 5, 2013).

4 Edward Felker, "Obama vows to be aggressive with regulation if Congress doesn't act," *Washington Guardian*, Energy Guardian, Feb. 13, 2013, http://www.washingtonguardian.com/one-tango (April 5, 2013).

5 James Madison, Alexander Hamilton, and John Jay, *The Federalist Papers* (New York: Barnes & Noble Classics, 2006), 277–78 (emphasis in original).

6 Ibid., 428.

7 *Dred Scott v. Sandford*, 60 U.S. 393 (1856).

8 *Plessy v. Ferguson*, 163 U.S. 537 (1896).

9 *Korematsu v. United States*, 323 U.S. 214 (1944).

10 "Fiscal Year 2013, Historical Tables, Budget of the U.S. Government," Office of Management and Budget, http://www.whitehouse.gov/sites/default/files/omb/budget/fy2013/assets/hist.pdf (March 17, 2013).

11 Ibid.

12 "CBO: Debt will be $7 trillion larger by 2023," *Daily Caller*, Feb. 6, 2013, http://dailycaller.com/2013/02/06/cbo-debt-to-increase-7-trillion-by-2023/ (April 5, 2013).

13 "Alert 496: Alert GAAP-Based U.S. Budget Deficit—Actual 2012 Federal Budget Deficit Hit $6.9 Trillion," American Business Analytics & Research LLC, Jan. 17, 2013, http://www.shadowstats.com/article/no-496-alert-gaap-based-us-budget-deficit (March 17, 2013).

14 Detlev Schlicter, "Bubble trouble: Is there an end to endless quantitative easing?" Feb. 22, 2013, http://detlevschlicter.com/2013/02/bubble-trouble-is-there-an-end-to-endless-quantitative-easing/ (April 5, 2013).

15 Editorial, "Mrs. Pelosi's VAT—The Speaker floats a middle-class tax hike," *Wall Street Journal*, Oct. 8, 2009, http://online.wsj.com/article/SB10001424052748703298004574457512007010416.html (March 17, 2013).

16 Elizabeth MacDonald, "Beware of Congress's Threat to Tax 401Ks," Fox Business, Oct. 31, 2008, http://www.foxbusiness.com/markets/2008/10/31/beware-congresss-threat-tax-ks/ (April 5, 2013).

17 Tocqueville, *Democracy in America*, 113.

18 Madison, *The Federalist*, 75.

19 Ibid., 259.

20 Ibid., 267.

21 U.S. Constitution, Art. V.

22 James Madison, *Notes of Debates in the Federal Convention of 1787* (Athens: Ohio University Press, 1985), 33.

23 Ibid., 105.

24 Ibid., 649.

25 Ibid.

26 Ibid., 610.

27 Madison, *The Federalist*, 246.

28 Robert G. Natelson, "The State-Application-and-Convention Method of Amending the Constitution: The Founding Era Vision," 29 *Thomas M. Cooley Law Review* 9 (2011).

29 The state legislatures can recommend specific language or amendments, but cannot seek to impose them through the application process as Article V empowers the delegates to the convention to propose amendments, which the states subsequently consider for ratification. The applications from the states must also be similar in subject area to reasonably conclude that two-thirds of the states are calling for a convention to address the same matters. See ibid.

30 Madison, *Notes on Debates*, 649.

31 Hamilton, *The Federalist*, 486.

2. An Amendment to Establish Term Limits for Members of Congress

1 "Historical Elections, Election Stats, 2010 cycle," Center for Responsive Politics, Opensecrets.org, http://www.opensecrets.org/bigpicture/elec_stats.php?cycle=2010 (April 18, 2013).

2 "Historical Elections, Election Stats, 2008 cycle," Center for Responsive Politics, Opensecrets.org, http://www.opensecrets.org/bigpicture/elec_stats.php?cycle=2008 (April 18, 2013).

3 Ronald Rotunda, "A Commentary on the Constitutionality of Term Limits," in *The Politics and Law of Term Limits*, Edward H. Crane and Roger Pilon, eds. (Washington, DC: Cato, 1994), 141.

4 Mark P. Petracca, "Restoring 'The University in Rotation': An Essay in Defense of Term Limitation," in *The Politics and Law of Term Limits*, Edward H. Crane and Roger Pilon, eds. (Washington DC: Cato, 1994), 74.

5 Pennsylvania Constitution, Section 8—September 28, 1776, http://avalon.law.yale.edu/18th_century/pa08.asp (April 18, 2013).

6 Pennsylvania Constitution, Section 19—September 28, 1776, http://avalon.law.yale.edu/18th_century/pa08.asp (April 18, 2013).

7 Articles of Confederation, Art. V, cl. 2, http://avalon.law.yale.edu/18th_century/artconf.asp (April 18, 2013).

8 James Madison, *Notes of Debates in the Federal Convention of 1787* (Athens: Ohio University Press, 1985), 52–53.

9 Petracca, "Restoring 'The University in Rotation,'" 60.

10 Thomas Jefferson, "Letter to James Madison, December 20, 1787," in *Memoir, Correspondence and Miscellanies, From the Papers of Thomas Jefferson*, 2nd ed., Thomas Jefferson Randolph, ed., vol. 2 (Boston: Gray & Bowen, 1830), http://www.gutenberg.org/dirs/1/6/7/8/16782/16782-h/16782-h.htm#link2H_4_0119 (April 18, 2013).

11 Jefferson, "Letter to Samuel Adams, February 26, 1800," in *Memoir, Correspondence and Miscellanies*, http://www.gutenberg.org/files/16783/16783-h/16783-h.htm#link2H_4_0258 (April 18, 2013).

12 Petracca, "Restoring 'The University in Rotation,'" 69–70.

13 U.S. Constitution, Twenty-Second Amendment.

14 Ibid.

15 Ibid.

16 *A Century of Lawmaking for a New Nation: U.S. Congressional Documents and Debates, 1774–1875*, Annals of Congress, House of Representatives, 1st Congress, 1st Session, July 16, 1789

(Library of Congress), 668–71, http://memory.loc.gov/cgi-bin /ampage?collId=llac&fileName=001/llac001.db&recNum=335.

17 Ibid., 671–74, http://memory.loc.gov/cgi-bin/ampage?collId=llac &fileName=001/llac001.db&recNum=337.

18 Ida A. Brudnick, "Salaries of Members of Congress: Recent Actions and Historical Tables," Congressional Research Service, Jan. 15, 2013, http://www.senate.gov/CRSReports/crs-publish.cfm ?pid='*2%404P%5C%5B%3A%22%40%20%20%0A (April 18, 2013).

19 "States with gubernatorial term limits," *Ballotpedia*, http://ballot pedia.org/wiki/index.php/States_with_gubernatorial_term_limits (April 18, 2013).

20 Virginia Constitution, Art. V, Section 1.

21 "Utah Set to Repeal Term Limits," National Conference of State Legislatures, March 26, 2003, http://www.ncsl.org/legislatures -elections/legisdata/utah-set-to-repeal-term-limits.aspx (April 18, 2013).

22 "The Term Limited States," National Conference of State Legislatures, January 2013, http://www.ncsl.org/legislatures-elections /legisdata/chart-of-term-limits-states.aspx (April 18, 2013).

23 Madison, *Notes of Debates*, 371.

24 Frank Newport, "Congress Approval Stagnant at Low Level," Gallup, Politics, March 11, 2013, http://www.gallup.com/poll/161210 /congress-approval-stagnant-low-level.aspx (April 18, 2013).

3. An Amendment to Restore the Senate

1 U.S. Constitution, Art. I, Section 3.

2 James Madison, *Notes of Debates in the Federal Convention of 1787* (Athens: Ohio University Press, 1985), 31.

3 Ibid., 40

4 Ibid., 41.

5 Ibid.

6 Ibid. Delegates from Vermont and New Hampshire had not yet arrived and taken their seats at the convention. Rhode Island chose to send no delegates to the convention and did not, in fact, ratify the Constitution until May 29, 1790. The rules the convention adopted prior to beginning deliberations required states to vote as a unit. If a majority of delegates from a state were unable to come to an agreement, that state's vote would be counted as divided.

7 Ibid.

8 Ibid., 41–42.

9 Ibid., 42.

10 *Debates in the Several State Conventions*, Jonathon Elliott, ed., vol. 1 (Philadelphia: Lippincott, 1901), 398.

11 Ibid., 399.

12 Ibid.

13 Ibid.

14 Rufus King, *The Life & Correspondence of Rufus King*, Charles R. King, ed., vol. 1 (New York: G. P. Putnam's Sons, 1894), 596.

15 Ibid., 597.

16 Ibid. (emphasis in original).

17 James Madison, Alexander Hamilton, and John Jay, *The Federalist Papers* (New York: Barnes & Noble Classics, 2006), 209.

18 Ibid., 213.

19 Pauline Maier, *Ratification—The People Debate the Constitution, 1787–1788* (New York: Simon & Schuster Paperbacks, 2010), 175.

20 Ibid., 177.

21 James Madison, "Speech in the Virginia Ratifying Convention in Defense of the Constitution," in *Writings*, Jack N. Rakove, ed. (New York: Library of America, 1999), 362–63.

22 Jay S. Bybee, "Ulysses at the Mast: Democracy, Federalism, and the Siren's song of the Seventeenth Amendment," 91 *Northwestern University Law Review* 500, 520 (1997). The practice of state legislatures issuing instructions to senators on pending legislation became almost ubiquitous before the ratification of the Seventeenth Amendment. In some cases, senators who believed that they could not, in good conscience, follow their instructions resigned or refused to stand for reelection later on. Suggestions were made by a few delegates to state conventions (at other times in congressional debates over changing the way senators were chosen) that it might be appropriate to give state legislatures the power to recall senators who failed to follow instructions, but the potential for malfeasance and abuse of that authority were self-evident and the subject was quickly abandoned. The only power the state legislature would have would be the right to deny the senator reelection.

23 Ibid., 536.

24 *Congressional Quarterly, Congressional Record* (various sources in each).

25 Ibid.

26 Brandon Stewart, "List of 27 States Suing Over Obamacare," Heritage Foundation, The Foundry blog, Jan. 17, 2011, http://blog.heritage.org/2011/01/17/list-of-states-suing-over-obama care/ (April 15, 2013).

27 "Republicans Make Historic Gains in State Legislatures, Pick Up Hundreds of Seats," FoxNews.com, Nov. 3, 2010, http://www.foxnews.com/politics/2010/11/03/republicans-make -historic-gains-state-legislatures-pick-hundreds-seats/ (April 15, 2013).

28 Sarah Torre, "Americans Continue to Oppose Obamacare's HHS Mandate," Heritage Foundation, The Foundry blog, April 11, 2013,

http://blog.heritage.org/2013/04/11/americans-continue-to-oppose
-obamacares-hhs-mandate/ (April 15, 2013).

4. An Amendment to Establish Term Limits for Supreme Court Justices and Super-Majority Legislative Override

1 U.S. Constitution, Art. III, Section 1.

2 U.S. Constitution, Art. I, Section 2.

3 James Madison, *Notes of Debates in the Federal Convention of 1787* (Athens: Ohio University Press, 1985), 61.

4 Ibid., 63.

5 James Madison, Alexander Hamilton, and John Jay, *The Federalist Papers* (New York: Barnes & Noble Classics, 2006), 428–29.

6 Robert Yates, "Brutus Essay No. 11," in *Anti-Federalist Papers and the Constitutional Convention Debates*, Ralph Ketcham, ed. (New York: Signet Classic, 2003), 293.

7 Yates, "Brutus Essay No. 15," in *Anti-Federalist Papers*, 308.

8 *Marbury v. Madison*, 5 U.S. 137, 178 (1803).

9 Thomas Jefferson, "Letter to Abigail Adams, September 11, 1804," in *The Writings of Thomas Jefferson*, Albert Ellery Bergh, ed., vol. 11 (Washington, DC: Thomas Jefferson Memorial Association of the United States, 1904), 50–51.

10 Thomas Jefferson, "Letter to William Charles Jarvis, September 28, 1820," in *The Writings of Thomas Jefferson*, Albert Ellery Bergh, ed., vols. 15–16 (Washington, DC: Thomas Jefferson Memorial Association of the United States, 1907), 277.

11 *Dred Scott v. Sanford*, 60 U.S. 393 (1857).

12 Carl Sandburg, *Abraham Lincoln: The War Years*, vol. 1 (New York: Harcourt, Brace & World, 1939), 132.

13 Woodrow Wilson, *Constitutional Government in the United States* (New York: Columbia University Press, 1908), 16.

14 Paul A. Rahe, "Progressive Racism," *National Review Online*, April 11, 2013, http://www.nationalreview.com/articles/345274 /progressive-racism-paul-rahe (April 18, 2013).

15 Robin L. West, *Re-Imagining Justice: Progressive Interpretations of Formal Equality, Rights, and the Rule of Law* (Burlington, VT: Ashgate, 2003), 9.

16 Franklin D. Roosevelt, "State of the Union Message to Congress, January 11, 1944," http://www.fdrlibrary.marist.edu/archives/address _text.html (April 18, 2013).

17 Bruce Ackerman, "Ackerman on Renewing the Promise of National Citizenship," March 15, 2005, American Constitution Society, ACS blog, http://www.acslaw.org/acsblog/ackerman-on-renewing -the-promise-of-national-citizenship (April 18, 2013).

18 Louis Michael Seidman, "Let's Give Up on the Constitution," *New York Times*, Dec. 30, 2012, http://www.nytimes.com/2012/12/31 /opinion/lets-give-up-on-the-constitution.html?pagewanted=all&_ r=2& (April 18, 2013).

19 Ruth Bader Ginsburg, "Lecture: Fifty-first Cardozo Memorial Lecture—Affirmative Action: An International Human Rights Dialogue," 21 *Cardozo Law Review* 253, 282 (1999).

20 Mark R. Levin and Andrew P. Zappia, "Seek and Ye Shall Find—Ginsburg's Philosophy," *New Jersey Law Journal*, July 12, 1993.

21 Interview with Justice Ruth Bader Ginsburg, Al-Hayat TV, Middle East Research Institute, January 30, 2012, http://www.memritv.org /clip_transcript/en/3295.htm.

22 *Thompson v. Oklahoma*, 487 U.S. 815, 830–831 (1988).

23 Stephen Breyer, "The Supreme Court and the New International Law," Speech to the American Society of International Law, Washington, D.C., April 4, 2003, http://www.supremecourt.gov

/publicinfo/speeches/viewspeeches.aspx?Filename=sp_04-04-03
.html (April 18, 2013).

24 *Lawrence v. Texas*, 539 U.S. 558, 572–573 (2003).

25 Sandra Day O'Connor, "Keynote Address Before the Ninety-Sixth Annual Meeting of the American Society of International Law," 96 *American Society of International Law Proceedings* 348, 350 (2002).

26 Sandra Day O'Connor, *The Majesty of the Law* (New York: Knopf, 2003).

27 Hope Yen, "O'Connor Extols Role of International Law," *Seattle Post-Intelligencer*, Oct. 27, 2004, http://www.ushumanrightsonline .net/news/article.62630-OConnor_extols_role_of_international_law (April 18, 2013).

28 Mark R. Levin, *Men in Black: How the Supreme Court Is Destroying America* (Washington, DC: Regnery, 2005), 22.

29 James Madison, "Letter to Henry Lee, June 25, 1824," in *Writings*, Jack N. Rakove, ed. (New York: Library of America, 1999), 803.

30 *Wickard v. Filburn*, 317 U.S. 111 (1942), *Everson v. Board of Education*, 330 U.S. 1 (1947), *Griswold v. Connecticut*, 381 U.S. 479 (1965), *Plyler v. Doe*, 457 U.S. 202 (1982), *Lawrence v. Texas*, 539 U.S. 558 (2003), *National Federation of Independent Business v. Sebelius*, 567 U.S. __ (2012).

31 *Dred Scott v. Sanford*, 60 U.S. 393 (1857), *Plessy v. Ferguson*, 323 U.S. 214 (1944), *Korematsu v. United States*, 323 U.S. 214 (1944), *Roe v. Wade*, 410 U.S. 113 (1973).

32 Levin, *Men in Black*, 1.

33 Ibid., 2–9 and accompanying citations.

34 James Madison, *The Writings of James Madison*, Gaillard Hunt, ed., vol. 5 (New York: G. P. Putnam's Sons, 1904), 184, http:// files.libertyfund.org/files/1937/Madison_1356-05_EBk_v6.0.pdf (April 19, 2013).

5. Two Amendments to Limit Federal Spending and Taxing

1 Milton Friedman, "Washington: Less Red Ink," *Atlantic*, February 1983, http://www.theatlantic.com/magazine/print/1983/02 /washinton-less-red-ink/305450/ (September 25, 2012).

2 Congressional Budget and Impoundment Control Act of 1974, Pub.L. 93–344, 88 Stat. 297, 2 U.S.C. §§ 601–688.

3 Ibid.

4 Chris Cox, "The con game we call Congress: In the still of the night, members raised pay, raided the Treasury," *Orange County Register*, November 26, 1989, p. 3G.

5 D. Andrew Austin and Mindy R. Levit, "The Debt Limit: History and Recent Increases," Congressional Research Service, Feb. 7, 2013, http://www.fas.org/sgp/crs/misc/RL31967.pdf (March 17, 2013).

6 "Fiscal Year 2013, Historical Tables, Budget of the U.S. Government," Office of Management and Budget, http://www.whitehouse .gov/sites/default/files/omb/budget/fy2013/assets/hist.pdf (March 17, 2013).

7 Ibid.

8 Ibid.

9 Keith Hennessey, "CBO's new deficit estimate," *Your Guide to American Economic Policy*, May 15, 2013, http://keithhennessey .com/2013/05/15/cbos-new-deficit-estimate/ (May 27, 2013). Therefore, the nation's fiscal situation remains grim and is getting much worse, only slightly slower, as large annual federal deficits continue to mount.

10 "NCSL Fiscal Brief: State Balanced Budget Provisions," National Conference of State Legislatures, October 2010, http://www.ncsl .org/documents/fiscal/statebalancedbudgetprovisions2010.pdf (March 17, 2013).

11 "Fiscal Year 2013, Historical Tables, Budget of the U.S. Government," Office of Management and Budget, http://www.whitehouse.gov/sites/default/files/omb/budget/fy2013/assets/hist.pdf (March 17, 2013).

12 "Debt Position and Activity Report," United States Department of the Treasury, http://www.treasurydirect.gov/govt/reports/pd/pd_debtposactrpt_1212.pdf (March 17, 2013).

13 Romina Boccia, "Obama: Don't Worry About $16 Trillion Debt," Heritage Foundation, The Foundry blog, Sept. 19, 2012, http://blog.heritage.org/2012/09/19/obama-dont-worry-about-16-trillion-debt/ (March 17, 2013).

14 "The 2012 Long-Term Budget Outlook," Congressional Budget Office, June 2012, http://www.cbo.gov/sites/default/files/cbofiles/attachments/06-05-Long-Term_Budget_Outlook_2.pdf (March 17, 2013).

15 "2012 Annual Report of the Boards of Trustees of the Federal Hospital Insurance and Federal Supplementary Medical Insurance Trust Funds," April 23, 2012, http://www.treasury.gov/resource-center/economic-policy/ss-medicare/Documents/TR_2012_Medicare.pdf (March 17, 2013).

16 "The 2012 Annual Report of the Board of Trustees of the Federal Old-Age and Survivors Insurance and Federal Disability Insurance Trust Funds," April 25, 2010, http://www.ssa.gov/oact/tr/2012/tr2012.pdf (March 17, 2013).

17 "Alert 496: Alert GAAP-Based U.S. Budget Deficit—Actual 2012 Federal Budget Deficit Hit $6.9 Trillion," American Business Analytics & Research LLC, Jan. 17, 2013, http://www.shadowstats.com/article/no-496-alert-gaap-based-us-budget-deficit (March 17, 2013).

18 Nikola G. Swann, "Research Update: United States of America Long-Term Rating Lowered to 'AA+' on Political Risks and Rising Debt

Burden; Outlook Negative," Standard & Poor's, Aug. 5, 2011, http://
www.standardandpoors.com/servlet/BlobServer?blobheadername
3=MDT-Type&blobcol=urldata&blobtable=MungoBlobs&blob
headervalue2=inline%3B+filename%3DUnitedStatesofAmerica
LongTermRatingLoweredToAA.pdf&blobheadername2=Content
-Disposition&blobheadervalue1=application%2Fpdf&blobkey=
id&blobheadername1=content-type&blobwhere=124394298773
3&blobheadervalue3=UTF-8 (March 17, 2013).

19 Nikola G. Swann, "Research Update: U.S. 'AA+/A-1+' Unsolicited
Ratings Affirmed; Outlook Remains Negative on Continued Political and Fiscal Risks," Standard & Poor's, June 8, 2012, http://www
.standardandpoors.com/servlet/BlobServer?blobheadername3=MDT
-Type&blobcol=urldata&blobtable=MungoBlobs&blobheader
value2=inline%3B+filename%3DUS_Unsolicited_Ratings_
Affirmed_6_8_12.pdf&blobheadername2=Content-Disposition
&blobheadervalue1=application%2Fpdf&blobkey=id&blob
headername1=content-type&blobwhere=1244131049439&blob
headervalue3=UTF-8 (March 17, 2013).

20 "The federal government's Long-Term Fiscal Outlook," Government Accountability Office, Fall 2012 Update, http://www.gao
.gov/assets/660/650466.pdf (March 17, 2013).

21 "What is the purpose of the Federal Reserve System?," Board of
Governors of the Federal Reserve, http://www.federalreserve.gov
/faqs/about_12594.htm (March 17, 2013).

22 Charles Kadlec, "The Federal Reserve's Explicit Goal: Devalue
the Dollar 33%," Forbes, Feb. 6, 2012, http://www.forbes.com
/sites/charleskadlec/2012/02/06/the-federal-reserves-explicit-goal
-devalue-the-dollar-33/ (April 8, 2013).

23 Jeff Cox, "Time Bomb? Bankers Pressured to Buy Government Debt,"
CNBC, May 31, 2012, http://www.cnbc.com/id/47633576/Time_

Bomb_Banks_Pressured_to_Buy_Government_Debt (March 17, 2013).

24 Alexis de Tocqueville, *Democracy in America*, Henry Reeve, trans., Phillips Bradley, ed., vol. 1 (New York: Library of America, 2004), 242.

25 Robert Yates, "Brutus Essay No. 6," *Debates on the Constitution*, vol. 1 (New York: Library of America, 1993), 618–19.

26 Ibid., "Brutus Essay No. 1," 166–67.

27 Ibid., 167.

28 James Madison, Alexander Hamilton, and John Jay, *The Federalist Papers* (New York: Barnes & Noble Classics, 1987), 230–31.

29 Joseph Story, *Commentaries on the Constitution of the United States*, 4th ed., Thomas M. Cooley, ed., vol. 1, §923 (Boston: Little, Brown, 1873) (citing Thomas Jefferson).

30 Amos Singletary, *Debates on the Constitution*, 906.

31 Ibid.

32 Ibid., 222, 225.

33 Story, *Commentaries*, §927.

34 Ibid., §909.

35 Ibid., §922.

36 Charlotte A. Twight, *Dependent on D.C.: The Rise of Federal Control Over the Lives of Ordinary Americans* (New York: Palgrave Macmillan, 2002), 99 (quoting House Committee on Ways and Means, Income Tax Letter from Commissioner of Revenue, 41st Cong., 3d sess., January 23, 1871, House Mis. Doc. No. 51, p. 1).

37 *Pollock v. Farmers' Loan & Trust Co.*, 157 U.S. 429 (1895).

38 "Federal Individual Income Tax Rates History," Tax Foundation, Sept. 9, 2011, http://taxfoundation.org/sites/taxfoundation.org/files /docs/fed_individual_rate_history_nominal%26adjusted-20110909 .pdf (March 17, 2013).

39 William McBride, "CBO Report Shows Increasing Redistribution in the Tax Code Despite No Long-term Trend in Income Inequality," Tax Foundation, July 24, 2012, http://taxfoundation.org/article /cbo-report-shows-increasing-redistribution-tax-code-despite-no -long-term-trend-income-inequality (April 11, 2013).

40 "The Distribution of Household Income and Federal Taxes, 2008 and 2009," Congressional Budget Office, July 2012, http://www.cbo .gov/sites/default/files/cbofiles/attachments/43373-06-11-House holdIncomeandFedTaxes.pdf (March 18, 2013).

41 "Putting a Face on America's Tax Return: Chart 29," Tax Foundation, Sept. 24, 2012, http://taxfoundation.org/article/putting-face -americas-tax-returns-chart-29 (March 17, 2013).

42 "Who Pays Income Taxes and How Much?," National Taxpayers Union, http://www.ntu.org/tax-basics/who-pays-income-taxes.html (March 17, 2013).

43 Scott A. Hodge, "No Country Leans on Upper-Income Households as Much as U.S.," Tax Foundation, March 21, 2011, http:// www.ntu.org/tax-basics/who-pays-income-taxes.html (March 17, 2013).

44 Isaac M. O'Bannon, "2003 Federal Income Tax Tables Released," CPA Practice Advisor, Jan. 15, 2013, http://www.cpapracticeadvisor .com/news/10853734/2013-federal-income-tax-tables-released (April 8, 2013).

45 Editorial, "Mrs. Pelosi's VAT—The Speaker floats a middle-class tax hike," Wall Street Journal, Oct. 8, 2009, http://online.wsj.com /article/SB10001424052748703298004574457512007010416 .html (March 17, 2013).

46 Sara Hansard, "House Democrats Contemplate Abolishing 401(k) Tax Breaks," Workforce Management, Oct. 16, 2008, updated Sept. 15, 2011, http://www.workforce.com/article/20081016

/NEWS01/310169987/house-democrats-contemplate-abolishing-401-k-tax-breaks# (March 17, 2013).

47 Joshua Green, "The Liberal Plan to End the Mortgage-Interest Deduction," *BloombergBusinessweek*, On Politics, Dec. 5, 2012, http://www.businessweek.com/articles/2012-12-05/the-liberal-plan-to-end-the-mortgage-interest-deduction (March 17, 2013).

48 Sarah Parnass, "Eliminating Charitable Deduction Would Help Budget, Hurt Charities," ABC News, Dec. 6, 2012, http://abcnews.go.com/Politics/OTUS/eliminating-charitable-deduction-budget-hurt-charities/story?id=17889183 (March 17, 2013).

49 Joel Griffith, "Krugman: U.S. Needs Death Panels, Sales Taxes," Breitbart, Feb. 5, 2013, http://www.breitbart.com/Big-Government/2013/02/04/Krugman-Death-panels-and-sales-taxes-is-how-we-do-this (March 17, 2013).

50 "2012 Annual Report to Congress," Internal Revenue Service, National Taxpayer Advocate, Dec. 31, 2012, http://www.taxpayeradvocate.irs.gov/userfiles/file/2012-Annual-Report-to-Congress-Executive-Summary.pdf (March 17, 2013).

51 James Bovard, "A Brief History of IRS Political Targeting," *Wall Street Journal*, May 14, 2013, http://online.wsj.com/article/SB10001424127887324715704578482823301630836.html (May 27, 2013).

52 *National Federation of Independent Business v. Sebelius*, 567 U.S. ___ (2012), Slip Op., No. 11-393, June 28, 2012.

53 Ibid. (Scalia, Kennedy, Thomas, and Alito, JJ. dissenting) (Slip Op., 24–25).

54 *Treasury Inspector General for Tax Administration Report, "Affordable Care Act: Planning Efforts for the Tax Provisions of the Patient Protection and Affordable Care Act Appear Adequate; However, the Resource Estimation Process Needs Improvement,"* Ref. No. 2012-

43-064, June 24, 2012, http://www.treasury.gov/tigta/auditreports/
2012reports/201243064fr.pdf.

55 I do not object to "the Fair Tax," which functions as a national
sales tax and eliminates all forms of revenue-based taxation, should
it be a preferred amendment by delegates to a state convention.
See "The Fair Tax Plan," Americans for Fair Taxation, http://www
.fairtax.org/site/PageServer?pagename=HowFairTaxWorks (April
8, 2013).

6. An Amendment to Limit the Federal Bureaucracy

1 U.S. Constitution, Art. I, Section 1.

2 James Madison, Alexander Hamilton, and John Jay, *The Federalist
Papers* (New York: Barnes & Noble Classics, 2006), 276–77.

3 Ibid., 275.

4 James Madison, "Debate in Virginia Ratifying Convention," in *The
Debates in the Several State Conventions on the Adoption of the Federal
Constitution*, 2nd ed., Jonathan Elliot, ed., vol. 3 (U.S. Congress,
1836), 514.

5 John Locke, *The Second Treatise of Government*, chap. 11, §141
(New York: Barnes & Noble, 2004).

6 Ibid.

7 Ibid., §134.

8 Ibid., §142.

9 Charles de Montesquieu, *The Spirit of the Laws*, Anne M. Cohler,
Basia C. Miller, and Harold S. Stone, eds., part 2, book 2, chapter 6
(Cambridge: Cambridge University Press, 2009).

10 Madison, *The Federalist Papers*, 288.

11 *Field v. Clark*, 143 U.S. 649, 692 (1892).

12 Woodrow Wilson, *Constitutional Government in the United States*
(New York: Columbia University Press, 1908), 56–57.

13 *Railroad Retirement Board v. Alton R. Co.*, 295 U.S. 330 (1935).

14 *Schechter Poultry Corp. v. United States*, 295 U.S. 495 (1935).

15 *Carter v. Carter Coal Co.*, 298 U.S. 238 (1936).

16 *Jones v. Laughlin Steel Corp.*, 301 U.S. 37 (1937).

17 *Wickard v. Filburn*, 317 U.S. 111 (1942).

18 James M. Landis, *The Administrative Process* (New Haven, CT: Yale University Press, 1938).

19 *Massachusetts v. Environmental Protection Agency*, 549 U.S. 497 (2007).

20 Nicole v. Crain & W. Mark Crain, "The Impact of Regulatory Costs on Small Firms," Small Business Administration, Office of Advocacy, September 2010, http://www.sba.gov/sites/default/files/The%20 Impact%20of%20Regulatory%20Costs%20on%20Small%20 Firms%20(Full).pdf (April 18, 2013).

21 "Piling On: The Year in Regulation," American Action Forum, Regulation, January 14, 2013, http://americanactionforum.org/ topic/piling-year-regulation (April 18, 2013).

22 Clyde Wayne Crews Jr., "Ten Thousand Commandments: An Annual Snapshot of the Federal Regulatory State—2012 Edition," Competitive Enterprise Institute, http://cei.org/sites/default/files /Wayne%20Crews%20-%2010,000%20Commandments%202012_0 .pdf (April 18, 2013).

23 Ibid.

24 Brian Walsh, "Overcriminalization: An Explosion of Federal Criminal Law," Heritage Foundation, April 27, 2011, http://www .heritage.org/research/factsheets/2011/04/overcriminalization-an -explosion-of-federal-criminal-law (April 18, 2013).

25 Barack Obama, "Remarks by the President in the State of the Union Address," White House, Feb. 12, 2013, http://www.whitehouse.gov

/the-press-office/2013/02/12/remarks-president-state-union-address
(April 18, 2013).

26 See generally, Administrative Procedure Act (5 U.S.C. § 553 et. seq.)

27 5 U.S.C. §801–802.

28 5 U.S.C. §706.

29 5 U.S.C. §706.

30 *Whitman v. American Trucking Associations Inc.*, 531 U.S. 457, 474 (2001).

31 *Chevron U.S.A. Inc. v. Natural Resources Defense Council, Inc.*, 467 U.S. 837 (1984). The legal doctrine takes its name from this case because this was the first time this particular regulatory interpretation was applied.

32 The Clean Air Act was officially enacted by Congress in 1963 as a research program. The 1970 amendments established the regulatory program pertaining to pollution thresholds.

33 Clean Air Act (CAA) §165(a)(1), §169(2)(c).

34 Clean Air Act (CAA) §169(1).

35 74 Fed. Reg. 55, 300-55, 303.

36 Patient Protection and Affordable Care Act, Pub. L. No. 111-148,124 Stat. 119, to be codified as amended at scattered sections of the Internal Revenue Code and in 42 U.S.C. (2010).

37 Peter Ferrara, *The Obamacare Disaster: An Appraisal of the Patient Protection and Affordable Care Act* (Chicago: Heartland Institute, 2010), v.

38 Curtis W. Copeland, "New Entities Created Pursuant to the Patient Protection and Affordable Care Act," Congressional Research Service, July 8, 2010, http://assets.opencrs.com/rpts/R41586_20110113.pdf (April 18, 2013).

39 "Obamacare Burden Tracker," House of Representatives Ways and

Means, Education and the Workforce, and Energy and Commerce
Committees, http://energycommerce.house.gov/sites/republicans
.energycommerce.house.gov/files/analysis/20120206ACATracker
.pdf (April 18, 2013).

40 Charlie Spiering, "Photo: 828 pages of new Obamacare regulations
in just one day," *Washington Examiner*, March 12, 2013, http://
washingtonexaminer.com/photo-828-pages-of-new-obamacare
-regulations-in-just-one-day/article/2524020 (April 18, 2013).

41 "IRS aims to clarify investment income tax under healthcare law,"
Reuters, Dec. 3, 2012, http://www.reuters.com/article/2012/12/03/
us-usa-tax-irs-idUSBRE8B21HA20121203.

42 Diane Cohen and Michael F. Cannon, "The Independent Payment
Advisory Board, PPACA's Anti-Constitutional and Authoritarian
Super-Legislature," Cato Institute, Policy Analysis, June 14, 2012,
http://www.cato.org/publications/policy-analysis/independent
-payment-advisory-board-ppacas-anticonstitutional-authoritarian
-superlegislature (April 18, 2013).

43 Dodd-Frank Wall Street Reform and Consumer Protection Act,
Pub.L. 111-203, H.R. 4173.

44 See 12 U.S.C. 5491 (2013).

45 12 U.S.C. 5491 et. seq. (2013).

46 See Complaint, *Competitive Enterprise Institute et. al. v. Timothy
Geithner et al.*, http://cei.org/sites/default/files/SNB%20v%20
Geithner%20-%20Complaint.PDF (April 18, 2013).

7. An Amendment to Promote Free Enterprise

1 U.S. Constitution, Art. I, Section 8.

2 Raoul Berger, "Judicial Manipulation of the Commerce Clause," 74
Texas Law Review 695, 702–703 (March, 1996) (internal citations
omitted).

3 Ibid., 704–705 (internal citations omitted).

4 Randy E. Barnett, "The Original Meaning of the Commerce Clause," 68 *University of Chicago Law Review* 101, 104 (Winter 2001) (emphasis in original).

5 Ibid., 114–15.

6 Ibid., 116.

7 Ibid.

8 Ibid., 124.

9 Robert H. Bork and Daniel E. Troy, "Locating the Boundaries: The Scope of Congress's Power to Regulate Commerce," 25 *Harvard Journal of Law & Public Policy* 849, 863–864 (Summer 2002).

10 James Madison, Alexander Hamilton, and John Jay, *The Federalist Papers* (New York: Barnes & Noble Classics, 2006), 235.

11 Ibid., 259.

12 According to the historian Andrew C. McLaughlin, "the cardinal principle of the Spanish colonial policy was monopoly and seclusion." Andrew C. McLaughlin, *The Confederation and the Constitution 1783–1789* (New York: Collier Books, 1962), 71. The British, furthermore, prohibited the importation of American whale oil to promote British fishing and restricted American shipping from the British West Indies. Ibid., 60–61.

13 Ibid., 86.

14 As a result, the framers specifically prohibited the states from issuing bills of credit, or to "make any Thing but gold and silver Coin a Tender in Payment of Debts" in Article I, Section 10 of the Constitution.

15 Joseph Story, *A Familiar Exposition of the Constitution of the United States*, §163 (Washington, DC: Regnery Gateway, 1986), 139–40.

16 Justice Thomas's concurring opinion in *United States v. Lopez*, 514 U.S. 549, 585–587 (1995), supports this understanding and

provides citations to the state ratification conventions. See, e.g., *Debates in the Several State Conventions on the Adoption of the Federal Constitution*, Jonathan Elliot, ed., vol. 2 (Washington, DC: United States Congress, 1836), 57 (T. Dawes at Massachusetts convention); ibid., 336 (M. Smith at New York convention).

17 See, e.g., *Federalist* 36: "Is the knowledge of local circumstances, as applied to taxation, a minute topographical acquaintance with all the mountains, rivers, streams, highways, and bypaths in each State; or is it a general acquaintance with its situation and resources . . . with the state of its *agriculture, commerce, manufactures* . . . with the nature of its products and consumptions . . . with the different degrees and kinds of its wealth, property, and industry?" *The Federalist Papers*, 188 (emphasis added). Hamilton distinguished between agriculture and commerce in *Federalist* 60: "The several States are in various degrees addicted to agriculture and commerce. In most, if not all of them, agriculture is predominant. In a few of them, however, commerce nearly divides its empire, and in most of them has a considerable share of influence." Ibid., 334. For a comprehensive analysis of the original meaning of the Commerce Clause and its terminology, see Randy E. Barnett, "The Original Meaning of the Commerce Clause," 68 *University of Chicago Law Review* 101 (Winter 2001).

18 The report from the participants, including Hamilton and Madison, stated that "the power of regulating trade is of such comprehensive extent, and will enter so far into the general System of the federal government, that to give it efficacy, and to obviate questions and doubts concerning its precise nature and limits, may require a correspondent adjustment of other parts of the Federal System." "Proceedings of Commissioners to Remedy Defects of the Federal Government, Sep. 11, 1786," in *The Debates on the Adoption of the Federal Constitution*, 2nd ed., Jonathan Elliot, ed., vol. 1 (New York: Burt Franklin, 1888), 118.

19 James Madison, "Vices of the Political System of the United States," in *Writings*, Jack N. Rakove, ed. (New York: Library of America, 1999), 71.

20 James Madison, *Notes of Debates in the Federal Convention of 1787* (Athens: Ohio University Press, 1985), 14.

21 Hamilton, *The Federalist Papers*, 63.

22 *Gibbons v. Ogden*, 22 U.S. 1, 190 (1824).

23 Ibid., 194–95 (emphasis added).

24 *Railroad Retirement Bd. v. Alton R. Co.*, 295 U.S. 330, 374 (U.S. 1935).

25 *A. L. A. Schechter Poultry Corp. v. United States*, 295 U.S. 495, 546 (1935).

26 *Carter v. Carter Coal Co.*, 298 U.S. 238, 308 (1936).

27 *NLRB v. Jones & Laughlin Steel Corp.*, 301 U.S. 1, 37 (1937).

28 *Wickard v. Filburn*, 317 U.S. 111 (1942).

29 Ibid., 128.

30 Ibid., 125.

31 *Maryland v. Wirtz*, 392 U.S. 183, 194 (1968).

32 Ibid., 198.

33 *Perez v. United States*, 402 U.S. 146, 154 (1971).

34 Ibid., 157.

35 *United States v. Lopez*, 514 U.S. 549, 558–559 (1995) (internal citations omitted).

36 Ibid., 619–20 (internal citations omitted).

37 Ibid., 614.

38 Ibid., 608.

39 Ibid., 574.

40 Ibid.

41 Berger, "Judicial Manipulation of the Commerce Clause," 715 (internal citations omitted).

42 *United States v. Morrison*, 529 U.S. 598, 617–618 (2000).

43 Ibid., 658–59.

44 *National Federation of Independent Business v. Sebelius*, 567 U.S. __ (2012) (internal citations omitted).

45 As an important aside, observe how judicial review today is mostly exercised to endorse expanded federal governmental authority.

46 Milton Friedman, *Capitalism and Freedom*, 40th anniversary ed. (Chicago: University of Chicago Press, 2002), 8.

8. An Amendment to Protect Private Property

1 John Locke, *The Second Treatise of Government*, Peter Laslett, ed., §138 (Cambridge: Cambridge University Press, 2003), 360.

2 William Blackstone, *Commentaries on the Laws of England*, 3rd ed., Thomas M. Cooley, ed., vol. 1 (Chicago: Callaghan, 1884), 138.

3 Ibid.

4 James Madison, Alexander Hamilton, and John Jay, *The Federalist Papers*, No. 54 (New York: Barnes & Noble Classics, 2006), 305.

5 Ibid.

6 Gouverneur Morris, "Political Enquiries," University of Chicago, *The Founders' Constitution*, Philip B. Kurland and Ralph Lerner, eds., ch. 16, doc. 8, http://press-pubs.uchicago.edu/founders/documents /v1ch16s8.html (April 18, 2013).

7 Ibid.

8 Ibid.

9 Virginia Declaration of Rights §1 (1776).

10 John Adams, "Defence of the Constitutions of Government of the United States," *The Founders' Constitution*, ch. 16, doc. 15, http:// press-pubs.uchicago.edu/founders/documents/v1ch16s15.html.

11 U.S. Constitution, Fifth Amendment.

12 See *Lucas v. South Carolina Coastal Council*, 505 U.S. 1003, 1028 (1992).

13 *Pennsylvania Coal Co. v. Mahon*, 260 U.S. 393, 415 (1922).

14 *Penn Central Transp. Co. v. New York City*, 438 U.S. 104, 124 (1978).

15 Ibid.

16 *Lucas v. South Carolina Coastal Council*, 505 U.S. 1003, 1017 n. 8 (1992).

17 *Concrete Pipe and Products of California, Inc. v. Construction Laborers Pension Trust for Southern California*, 508 U.S. 602, 645 (1993).

18 *Lingle v. Chevron U.S.A. Inc.*, 544 U.S. 528, 538–539 (2005) (citing in part *Penn Central Transp. Co. v. New York City*, 438 U.S. 104, 124 (1978)).

19 "Executive Order 12630: Governmental actions and interference with constitutionally protected property rights," 53 Fed. Reg. 8859 (March 18, 1988).

20 Report, "Regulatory Takings Implementation of Executive Order on Government Actions Affecting Private Property Use," Government Accountability Office, September 2003, http://www.gao.gov/assets/240/239832.pdf (April 18, 2013).

9. An Amendment to Grant the States Authority to Directly Amend the Constitution

1 U.S. Constitution, Art. V.

2 "Measures Proposed to Amend the Constitution," United States Senate, http://www.senate.gov/pagelayout/reference/three_column_table/measures_proposed_to_amend_constitution.htm (April 18, 2013).

3 Woodrow Wilson, *Constitutional Government in the United States* (New York: Columbia University Press, 1908), 16.

4 Ibid., 57.

5 U.S. Constitution, Tenth Amendment.

6 Mark R. Levin, *Liberty and Tyranny* (New York: Threshold Editions, 2009), 56.

7 Ibid. (citing *Prigg v. Pennsylvania*, 41 U.S. 539 [1842] and *Dred Scott v. Sanford*, 60 U.S. 393 [1857]).

8 *Plessy v. Ferguson*, 163 U.S. 537 (1896).

9 Charles Paul Freund, "Dixiecrats Triumphant: The Menacing Mr. Wilson," *Reason*, Dec. 18, 2002, http://reason.com/archives /2002/12/18/dixiecrats-triumphant (April 18, 2013).

10 Abraham Lincoln, "Speech at Lewistown, Illinois, Aug. 17, 1858," in *The Collected Works of Abraham Lincoln*, vol. 2 (New Brunswick, NJ: Rutgers University Press, 1953), 546–47.

11 William P. Ruger and Jason Sorens, "Freedom in the 50 States: Third Edition (2013)," Mercatus Center, April 2013, http://freedom inthe50states.org/download/Freedom_50_States_2013_summary .pdf (April 11, 2013).

12 James Madison, Alexander Hamilton, and John Jay, *The Federalist Papers* (New York: Barnes & Noble Classics, 2006), 213–14.

13 Ibid., 259.

14 "Massachusetts Ratification Convention, Feb. 6, 1788," in *Founding America: Documents from the Revolution to the Bill of Rights* (New York: Barnes & Noble, 2006), 591.

15 Ibid., 592–93.

16 Ibid., "Virginia Ratification Convention, June 27, 1788," 594.

17 Ibid., 595–97.

18 Ibid., "New York Ratification Convention, July 26, 1788," 601–604.

19 James Madison, "Speech to Congress Proposing Constitutional Amendments," in *Writings*, Jack N. Rakove, ed. (New York: Library of America, 1999), 438.

20 Ibid., 449.

21 Mark R. Levin, *Ameritopia* (New York: Threshold Editions, 2011), 185–86.

22 Levin, *Liberty and Tyranny*, 193.

23 Madison, *The Federalist Papers*, 288.

24 U.S. Constitution, Art. V.

25 Madison, *Writings*, 364.

10. An Amendment to Grant the States Authority to Check Congress

1 Joseph Story, *Commentaries on the Constitution of the United States*, vol. 3, §1821, University of Chicago, *The Founders' Constitution*, Philip B. Kurland and Ralph Lerner, eds., http://press-pubs.uchicago.edu/founders/documents/a5s12.html (April 19, 2013).

2 Peter James Stanlis, *Edmund Burke: The Enlightenment and Revolution* (Edison, NJ: Transaction, 1991), 213, citing Edmund Burke, "A Letter to a Noble Lord," in *Works*, vol. 5 (Boston: Little, Brown, 1904), 186.

3 John Adams, "Letter to Thomas Jefferson, November 13, 1815," in *The Adams-Jefferson Letters: The Complete Correspondence Between Thomas Jefferson and Abigail and John Adams*, Lester J. Cappon, ed. (Chapel Hill: University of North Carolina Press, 1959), 456.

4 Thomas Jefferson, "Letter to James Madison, December 20, 1787," in *The Debate on the Constitution* (New York: Library of America, 1993), 213.

5 Peter Roff, "Pelosi: Pass Health Reform So You Can Find Out What's In It," *U.S. News & World Report*, Politics blog, March 9, 2010, http://www.usnews.com/opinion/blogs/peter-roff/2010/03/09/pelosi-pass-health-reform-so-you-can-find-out-whats-in-it (April 19, 2013).

6 U.S. Constitution, Art. I, Section 7, Cl. 2.

7 Draft Complaint for Declaratory and Injunctive Relief, Landmark Legal Foundation, http://www.landmarklegal.org/uploads

/Landmark%20Complaint%20(00013086-2).pdf (April 18, 2013).

8 Shailagh Murray, "On Hill, Clinton gives a health care pep talk," *Washington Post*, Nov. 11, 2009, http://articles.washingtonpost .com/2009-11-11/politics/36893630_1_health-care-bill-bill-clinton -senate-floor (April 19, 2013).

9 "Dodd-Frank, Still Wrong for America," Heritage Foundation, Fact Sheet 108, July 17, 2012, http://www.heritage.org/research /factsheets/2012/07/dodd-frank-still-wrong-for-america (April 19, 2013).

10 Amy Payne, "Morning Bell: Dodd-Frank Financial Regulations Strangling Economy," Heritage Foundation, The Foundry blog, July 20, 2012, http://blog.heritage.org/2012/07/20/morning-bell -dodd-frank-financial-regulations-strangling-economy/ (April 19, 2013).

11 Ammon Simon, "Dodd-Frank at Two: Bad for Business and the Constitution," *National Review Online*, Bench Memos, July 25, 2012, http://www.nationalreview.com/bench-memos/312267 /dodd-frank-two-bad-business-and-constitution-ammon-simon (April 19, 2013).

12 Jonathan Weisman, "Spending Measure Not a Law, Suit Says," *Washington Post*, March 22, 2006, http://www.washingtonpost .com/wp-dyn/content/article/2006/03/21/AR2006032101763.html (April 19, 2013).

13 S.47: Violence Against Women Reauthorization Act of 2013, http:// www.govtrack.us/congress/bills/113/s47/text (April 19, 2013).

14 Eugene Volokh, "Senate Considering Extending Statute That Led to Unconstitutional Prosecution for Twitter Messages That Criticized Religious Leader," Volokh Conspiracy, April 24, 2012, http://www .volokh.com/2012/04/24/senate-considering-extending-statute

-that-led-to-unconstitutional-prosecution-for-twitter-messages
-that-criticized-religious-leader/ (April 19, 2013); Wendy Ka-
miner, "What's Wrong with the Violence Against Women Act,"
Atlantic, March 19, 2012, http://www.theatlantic.com/national
/archive/2012/03/whats-wrong-with-the-violence-against-women
-act/254678/ (April 19, 2013); Hans Bader, "Troubling Provisions
Being Added to the Violence Against Women Act: Due Process
Rights Threatened," Competitive Enterprise Institute, OpenMarket
.org, March 23, 2012, http://www.openmarket.org/2012/03/23
/troubling-provisions-being-added-to-the-violence-against-women
-act-due-process-rights-threatened/ (April 19, 2013).

15 Daniel Horowitz, "Say No to Violence Against Constitution Act,"
RedState, April 23, 2012, http://www.redstate.com/dhorowitz3
/2012/04/23/say-no-to-violence-against-the-constitution-act
/ (April 19, 2013).

16 *U.S. v. Morrison*, 529 U.S. 598 (2000).

17 John Adams, "Letter to Thomas Jefferson, November 13, 1815,"
in *The Adams-Jefferson Letters*, 456.

18 Edmund Burke, "Letters on a Regicide Peace, Letter II, On the
Genius and Character of the French Revolution as it regards other
Nations," in *The Works of the Right Honorable Edmund Burke*, vol. 2
(London: Holdsworth & Ball, 1841), 315.

19 Thomas Jefferson, "Letter to Arthur Campbell, September 1,
1797," in *The Works of Thomas Jefferson*, Federal ed., vol. 8
(New York & London: G. P. Putnam's Sons, 1904–1905), http://
oll.libertyfund.org/?option=com_staticxt&staticfile=show
.php%3Ftitle=805&chapter=87108&layout=html&Itemid=27
(April 19, 2013).

11. An Amendment to Protect the Vote

1 *Crawford v. Marion County Election Board*, 472 F.3d 949, 953 (6th Cir. 2007), aff'd, 553 U.S. 181 (2008).

2 Ibid.

3 Ibid.

4 Scott Rasmussen, "64 Percent See Voter Fraud as a Serious Problem," *Rasmussen Reports*, April 18, 2012, http://www.rasmussenreports .com/public_content/most_recent_podcasts/2012_04/radio_update _64_percent_see_voter_fraud_as_a_serious_problem (April 20, 2013).

5 *Crawford v. Marion County Election Board*, 553 U.S. 181, 204 (2008).

6 Ibid.

7 Mary Sanchez, "Will Republicans succeed with Jim Crow lite laws?" *Kansas City Star*, Sept. 3, 2012, http://www.kansascity.com /2012/09/03/3790385/voter-id-laws.html#storylink=cpy (April 20, 2013).

8 Adam Crisp, "Jesse Jackson 'Astonished' by Haley's Voter ID Views," *Mount Pleasant Patch*, Sept. 3, 2012, http://mountpleasant-sc.patch .com/articles/jesse-jackson-astonished-by-haley-s-voter-id-views (April 20, 2013).

9 Amy Bingham, "Eric Holder Dubs Texas Voter ID Law a 'Poll Tax,'" ABC News, July 10, 2012, http://abcnews.go.com/blogs /politics/2012/07/eric-holder-dubs-texas-voter-id-law-a-poll-taxes / (April 20, 2013). It is important to note that Holder's use of the term "poll taxes" was a departure from his prepared remarks. See Eric Holder, "Attorney General Eric Holder Speaks at the NAACP Annual Convention," July 10, 2012, http://www.justice .gov/iso/opa/ag/speeches/2012/ag-speech-120710.html (April 20, 2013).

10 Katie Pavlich, "NAACP Requires Photo I.D. to See Holder Speak in State Being Sued Over Voter ID," Townhall.com, The Tipsheet, July 10, 2012, http://townhall.com/tipsheet/katie pavlich/2012/07/10/naacp_requires_photo_id_to_see_holder_speak (April 20, 2013).

11 Karen Langley, "Voter ID passes Pennsylvania Senate," *Pittsburgh Post-Gazette*, March 8, 2012, http://www.post-gazette.com/stories /local/state/voter-id-passes-pa-senate-221495/?print=1 (April 20, 2013).

12 "PA Voter ID," NAACP Pennsylvania State Conference, http:// pastatenaacp.org/voting/pa-voter-id/ (April 20, 2013).

13 Anson Asaka, "The Fight Against Voter Suppression in Pennsylvania," NAACP blog, September 14, 2012, http://www.naacp.org /blog/entry/the-fight-against-voter-suppression-in-pennsylvania (April 20, 2013).

14 Corey Dade, "Judge refuses to block Pennsylvania Voter ID law," NPR, It's All Politics blog, Aug. 15, 2012, http://www.npr.org /blogs/itsallpolitics/2012/08/15/158827591/judge-refuses-to-block -pa-voter-id-law-appeal-headed-to-state-supreme-court (April 20, 2013).

15 Ibid.

16 Amy Davidson, "Pennsylvania's Voter ID Law Delayed," *New Yorker*, Close Read, October 2, 2012, http://www.newyorker.com /online/blogs/closeread/2012/10/pennsylvanias-voter-id-law -delay.html.

17 Ariz. Rev. Stat. §16-166(F).

18 *Gonzalez v. Arizona*, 677 F.3d 383 (9th Cir. 2012).

19 John Fund and Hans von Spakovsky, *Who's Counting? How Fraudsters and Bureaucrats Put Your Vote at Risk* (New York: Encounter Books, 2012).

20 *Gonzalez v. Arizona*, 435 F. Supp. 2d 997 (D.Ariz. 2006).

21 *Gonzalez v. Arizona*, 677 F.3d 383 (9th Cir. 2012).

22 *Arizona v. The Inter Tribal Council of Arizona*, 570 U.S. __ (2013).

23 Alexander Keyssar, *The Right to Vote: The Contested History of Democracy in the United States* (New York: Basic Books, 2009), 4.

24 Ibid., Table A.2.

25 Ibid.

26 Ibid.

27 Ibid.

28 U.S. Constitution, Art. I, Section 2.

29 U.S. Constitution, Art. I, Section 4. The Seventeenth Amendment, ratified in 1913, provided for the direct election of senators.

30 U.S. Constitution, Art. II, Section 1, Cl. 2 and U.S. Constitution, Twelfth Amendment.

31 Joseph Story, *Commentaries on the Constitution of the United States,* Thomas M. Cooley, ed., vol. 2, §820 (Clark, NJ: Lawbook Exchange, 2011).

32 James Madison, Alexander Hamilton, and John Jay, *The Federalist Papers* (New York: Barnes & Noble Classics, 2006), 292–93.

33 *The Anti-Federalist Papers*, Ralph Ketcham, ed. (New York: Signet Classic, 1983), 220 (emphasis added).

34 Ibid., 225.

35 Dumas Malone, *Jefferson: The Virginian* (Boston: Little, Brown, 1948), 379–80.

36 Keyssar, *The Right to Vote*, Table A.3.

37 Ibid. (New York's property requirement applied only "to men of color"; Rhode Island and North Carolina generally applicable property requirements).

38 Ibid.

39 Ibid., Table A.9.

40 Civil Rights Act of 1964, Pub. L. No. 88-352, 78 Stat. 241, Voting Rights Act of 1965, Pub. Law 89-110, 79 Stat. 437.

41 Section 5, Voting Rights Act, 47 U.S.C. §1973c (2012).

42 Ibid.

43 Voting Rights Act of 1965, Pub. Law 89-110, 79 Stat. 437.

44 "About Section 5 of the Voting Rights Act," United States Department of Justice, http://www.justice.gov/crt/about/vot/sec_5/about.php (April 20, 2013).

45 "Section 2 of the Voting Rights Act," United States Department of Justice, http://www.justice.gov/crt/about/vot/sec_2/about_sec2.php (April 20, 2013).

46 Voting Rights Act Amendments of 2006, Public Law 109-246, 120 Stat. 577.

47 Ibid.

48 *Shelby County v. Holder*, 570 U.S. __ (2013).

49 42 U.S.C. § 1973gg and 42 U.S.C. § 15301–15545 (2013).

50 John Fund and Hans von Spakovsky, *Who's Counting? How Fraudsters and Bureaucrats Put Your Vote at Risk* (New York: Encounter Books, 2012).

51 Ibid., 88.

52 Ibid., 87.

53 Ibid., 86 (citing Government Accountability Office, "Elections: Additional Data Could Help State and Local Election Officials Maintain Accurate Voter Registration Lists," 42 (2005)).

54 Ibid., (citing "The 2010 Election: A Look Back at What Went Right and Wrong," statement of Colorado Secretary of State Scott Gessler before the Committee on House Administration, 112th Congress [2011]).

55 "Inaccurate, Costly, and Inefficient," Pew Center on the States, Issue Brief, February 2012, http://www.pewtrusts.org/uploadedFiles

/wwwpewtrustsorg/Reports/Election_reform/Pew_Upgrading
_Voter_Registration.pdf (April 20, 2013).

56 Ibid.

57 Ibid.

58 U.S. Constitution, Art. I, Section 4, Cl. 1.

59 U.S. Constitution, Art. II, Section 1, Cl. 2.

60 U.S. Constitution, Art. II, Section 1, Cl. 4.

61 U.S. Constitution, Fifteenth Amendment.

62 U.S. Constitution, Nineteenth Amendment.

63 U.S. Constitution, Twenty-Fourth Amendment.

64 U.S. Constitution, Twenty-Sixth Amendment.

Epilogue: The Time for Action

1 Franklin D. Roosevelt, *Whither Bound?* (Boston: Houghton Mifflin, 1926).

2 Ibid., 15–16.

3 "State Governments Viewed Favorably as Federal Rating Hits New Low," Pew Research Center for the People and the Press, April 15, 2013, http://www.people-press.org/2013/04/15/state-govermnents-viewed-favorably-as-federal-rating-hits-new-low/ (April 19, 2013).

4 Abraham Lincoln, "The Gettysburg Address," Nov. 19, 1863, http://www.abrahamlincolnonline.org/lincoln/speeches/gettysburg.htm (April 19, 2013).

5 Russell L. Caplan, *Constitutional Brinksmanship* (New York: Oxford University Press, 1988), 74 (citing *Washington Post*, May 27, 1963, at 22). There are several excellent resources that provide further background and advice on the state convention process, including but not limited to Robert G. Natelson's writings. See Robert G. Natelson, "Amending the Constitution by Convention: A Complete View of the Founders' Plan (Part 1 in a series)," Goldwater

Institute, Sept. 16, 2010, http://www.goldwaterinstitute.org/article
/amending-constitution-convention-complete-view-founders-plan
-part-1-series (April 19, 2013); Robert G. Natelson, "Learning
from Experience: How the States Used Article V Applications
in America's First Century (Part 2 in a series)," Goldwater Institute, Nov. 4, 2010, http://goldwaterinstitute.org/sites/default
/files/Final%20110310%2C%20Article%20V%20Part%202%20
FINAL.pdf (April 19, 2013); Robert G. Natelson, "Amending the
Constitution by Convention: Practical Guidance for Citizens and
Policymakers (Part 3 in a three-part series)," Goldwater Institute,
http://goldwaterinstitute.org/sites/default/files/PB%2011-02%20
Article%20V%20Part%203%20of%203_0.pdf (April 19, 2013).

6 Ibid., 88 (citing 23 Weekly Compilation of Presidential Documents
766 (1987)).

7 Ronald Reagan, *A Time for Choosing: The Speeches of Ronald
Reagan—1961–1982* (Chicago: Regnery Gateway, 1983), 57.